Rural Unrest in Nepal

A History of Resistance, Revolt and Rebellion

Rural Unrest in Nepal

A History of Resistance, Revolt and Rebellion

David Seddon

with Jagat Basnet & Suresh Dhakal

ADROIT

Adroit Publishers

NEW DELHI • KATHMANDU

ISBN : 978-81-87393-88-7

2020

Published by
ADROIT PUBLISHERS 4675/21, Ganpati Bhawan, Ansari Road,
Daryaganj, New Delhi-110 002 Phone : 011-23266030
adroitpublishers@gmail.com

Typeset in Garamond Premier Pro by Arun, Akriti Graphic Solution, Delhi-110081 E-mail: arun263923@gmail.com, Ph: 9999414390

Preface

In 1994, Pratyoush Onta reviewed the 'rich possibilities' for a social history of Nepal, and commented that 'as Krishna Ghimire says in his recent book, social movements in Nepal are poorly documented' (1992: 138-146). He adds that 'scattered references to individual and collective acts of open resistance during Rana and Shah rule are found, but no substantive effort has been made to examine these' (Onta 1994: 3). A decade later, in their introduction to 'The People's War in Historical Context', the editors remarked that 'there is a long but largely undocumented history of popular uprisings and revolts against the autocratic rulers of Nepal…' (Karki & Seddon 2003: 3), despite the fact that Karki himself had written extensively on 'movements from below' in his PhD thesis and in an article published in 2002 (Karki 2002).

Ten years later, Suresh Dhakal remarked that 'rural social movements are poorly documented in Nepal. Rural clashes have not entered the public domain unless they involved large-scale participation or significant casualties' (Dhakal 2013: 131). Dhakal himself attempted to document such 'small rural clashes' in his historical analysis of a movement that started in Kanara, in Bardiya District, and later spread throughout the district and adjoining areas, as part of a more wide-ranging study of 'land tenure, agrarian relations and peasant movements in Nepal' (Dhakal 2013), and Jagat Basnet has also written on land rights and peasant movements in Nepal (eg Upreti, Sharma & Basnet 2008: 19-57).

Since these, there have been several more recent contributions, to which we shall refer in the course of this book, which is an attempt to bring together in one place what is known regarding the various forms of rural unrest - including resistance, rebellion, revolt and revolution - that characterize the history of Nepal from the earliest times to the present. One of the most recent attempts to bring this body of historical and anthropological data together was published recently as a chapter by David Seddon in a collection on '*Peasant Studies in Nepal*' (edited by Laya Prasad Uprety, Suresh Dhakal and Jagat Basnet (2018). This book builds on that work.

All of those involved in this book have worked for many years on issues associated with the political economy of agrarian change, peasant movements and rural unrest. They owe a debt to the many social scientists and political activists who have studied the same issues and have thus laid a foundation for this new compilation and synthesis, but they also wish to acknowledge, recognize and celebrate here the crucial role of those who were involved - as leaders, organizers and participants - in the hundreds of acts of defiance and resistance, and attempts to improve the lot of small farmers, peasants and rural workers in Nepal over the decades, initiatives that remain, after all, inadequately recorded and re-told, even now.

Kathmandu, Nepal & Brockdish, Norfolk, UK
June 2020

Contents

Introduction

The Focus of this Book

In his review of 'political violence in Nepal', John Whelpton notes that, in 1850, Jang Bahadur Rana told Orfeur Cavenagh that 'although revolutions often occurred (in Nepal), yet the country as a whole did not suffer more from such disturbances than England would from a change of Ministry; neither the army nor the peasantry taking any part in the disputes, and submitting without a murmur to the dictates of whichever party might emerge the victors' (Whelpton 2013: 27). The notion that 'revolutions' in Nepal were essentially the result of struggles between factions at the national level, without the involvement of the army or the peasantry, is one that tends to be perpetuated in the 'histories of the Ranas' (mainly by Ranas - see bibliography) which tend to focus on palace and court intrigue, and on factional divisions within the ruling class.

Careful study suggests, however, that in reality, the regime over which Jang Bahadur and his Rana successors presided for many years (1846-1951) was indeed subject to various forms of violence and conflict in which not only the peasantry but also the army was involved. Furthermore, the previous 'pre-Rana' regime under Bhimsen Thapa (from 1816 to 1846) also experienced rebellion and revolt even after the 'unification' of the Gorkhali State; while the earlier process of 'unification' (from 1743 to 1793) itself involved protracted rural conflict, including various forms of resistance and rebellion, arising from the reluctance of many of the petty states and tribal chiefdoms across the western, central and eastern hills to recognize or to submit to the authority and rule of the emerging Gorkhali state. Even before 'unification', furthermore, there is some evidence of rural conflict both between and within those petty states that preceded the rise of the state of Gorkha.

In this book, we will examine the history of rural unrest over a period of some three centuries, firstly, in the context of the history of the rise of Gorkha and the 'unification' and development of the Gorkhali State, initially under the Shah rulers of what was formerly one of several petty hill states (Gorkha) and subsequently under the dynasty of hereditary prime ministers, the Ranas. Then, we shall consider the more recent period following the overthrow of the Ranas, from 1951 up to the 1990s.

We shall not consider here the last twenty-five years following the launching of the ten year long Maoist insurgency or 'People's War' (1996-2006). We hope to be able to treat this period, which began with what the Maoists and their followers regarded at the time as a revolutionary struggle to overthrow the existing political, economic and social order to establish 'a new Nepal', in a future work, as a kind of sequel.

In this book we will explore the differences and the relationships between various forms of rural unrest, including: resistance to incorporation within the state; revolts against the imposition of excessive tithes and taxes by the state and against demands for rent by landowners and overlords; and rebellions against the authority and jurisdiction of the state. We shall not, as we have already indicated, address recent attempts at revolutionary change, leaving this to another time.

The Peasantry and Rural Unrest

There is a substantial literature on 'the peasantry' and on the defining characteristics of peasant economy, society and politics, which we shall not rehearse here; but Eric Wolf, in his *Peasant Wars of the Twentieth Century,* neatly defined 'peasants' as rural dwellers who broadly are subject to 'the dictates of a super-ordinate state' (Wolf 1973: xviii). Others have tried, often misleadingly, to distinguish 'peasants', who are by this definition generally subordinate to the state, from 'tribal' communities, that are often said to live effectively beyond 'the pale', and thus to be generally not subject to state control. In Nepal, some authors have described these 'tribal' social formations, again somewhat misleadingly, as '*adhivasi*' (indigenous).

However, we would suggest that the distinction between 'tribes' and 'peasants' has more to do with the specifics of political as well as of social and economic organization than with whether they are beyond or within the boundaries of the state. Many pre-capitalist agrarian states were historically able to maintain effective control over the rural population only under certain circumstances. The varying limits to that control defined, at any one time, the physical boundaries between those areas where the local rural population was subject to state control and those areas where it was not (and constituted various forms of 'tribal' or '*adhivasi*' economy and society) and also determined the extent and precise delineation of the 'marginal areas' between these two, where 'bandits' and outlaws often operated[1].

1. For example, the 'water margins' of the Huainan region of mediaeval China, where the outlaw Song Jiang and his 36 companions were active during the 11th century CE, or the areas of *siba* (dissidence) in pre-colonial Morocco, where various forms of rural unrest, including rebellions against the *makhzen* (the state) have been identified (Seddon 1978).

Even in modern states, the peasantry may resist specific dictates of, or interventions by, the state, by a variety of means, including the deployment of what James Scott has called 'the weapons of the weak' (Scott 1985); which may involve negotiation with the authorities, fleeing to escape the jurisdiction of the authorities, or, where these actions or reactions are not possible or fail, even revolt (see Wolf 1973). This, of course, does not make them 'tribes'.

Distinct, in our view, from peasant uprisings or revolts – which are movement of unrest from below that are usually responses of 'the last resort' to particular circumstances in which a material or moral contract is felt to have been broken[2] – are 'rebellions', which are generally led by local notables, and effectively challenge or refuse the authority of a particular regime, or even of the state more generally. When rebellion effectively threatens the regime, it may well overlap with what Whelpton has called 'elite politics'. Finally, all forms of rural unrest may appear as 'ethnic unrest' where those involved can be clearly defined by the tribal or ethnic identity and common interests as such, or else themselves invoke their membership of a distinct tribal or ethnic group as a crucial element in their struggle.

In his discussion of 'political violence in Nepal', Whelpton distinguishes four main types of what he calls 'politically motivated violence': conflicts within the political elites, ethnic and regional resistance, agrarian revolt, and 'crusades'. He argues that the first of these – conflicts within the elite - coincides pretty much with Jung Bahadur's own view 'that a successful replacement of the top power holders was always an elite affair, and that the mass of the population meekly accepted the dictates of the victor' – commenting that this was 'of course, an oversimplified view but

2. As when rents, taxes or consumer prices rise 'unreasonably' (see Walton & Seddon 1994 with reference to urban protest).

not too far out of line with the situation in the mid-nineteenth century' (Whelpton 2013: 28). It could be argued, we suggest, that formal politics continued to be an elite affair for the most part under the Ranas, well into the first half of the 20th century and, indeed, arguably even thereafter up to the present time, despite the claim that Nepal is (at least since the Jana Andolan of 1990 and subsequent revision of the Constitution) a democracy.

Elite politics are often characterized, as has previously been suggested, as 'ethnic' or 'regional' politics in which the claim is made, either by commentators and analysts or else by members of a disaffected or marginalized elite, that they represent a disadvantaged or oppressed ethnic (eg Limbu) or regional (eg Madheshi) population. Ethnic and regional unrest, however, need not be a function of elite politics, in so far as elements of the rural population may also define themselves, when involved in various forms of rural unrest, less in class terms than in terms of ethnicity or some other form of identity, including that of a particular region (eg 'the Jhapa uprising').

Whelpton seems at least initially to associate 'ethnic unrest' particularly with the circumstances of what he calls 'the original Gorkha conquest', although he accepts that 'there were, however, rather more instances of ethnically based revolts in the intervening years than is sometimes perceived' (ibid.). It is also the case that rural conflict in the long period from 1790 to 1990 also often presented itself to some extent at least as ethnic conflict, while, in the aftermath of the Jana Andolan of 1990 and the rise of identity politics, ethnicity became – and effectively continues to be - the dominant frame of reference for conflict and unrest, for many observers as well as for those involved. This tends, however, to encourage the conflation of elite politics with ethnic politics, class-based divisions and rural unrest.

The extent to which a rural uprising or movement may be identified as 'ethnic' depends, I suggest, on a number of factors, including the characterization of the uprising or movement both by outsiders and by the participants themselves. But uprisings and movements identified (by the participants and/or outside commentators) as 'ethnic' certainly did not end in the late 18th and early 19th century CE; they have also been a feature of rural conflict in both the 20th and 21st centuries CE. Indeed, there has been a dominant tendency in Nepal studies as a whole, as well as in common parlance, particularly in recent years, to define political, social and economic relations exclusively in terms of caste and ethnicity when, in reality other aspects of social identity, like class, have played a crucial part – indeed, we would argue a determinant part.

As regards 'agrarian revolt', Whelpton comments that 'tensions between the peasantry and those claiming a share of their produce as rent or taxation could result in violence and, where both cultivator and landlord were from the same ethnic group, this could be seen as straightforward class conflict. However, in particular areas, matters were more complex, as the agrarian divide coincided with an ethnic one' (Whelpton 2013: 28) - the point made above. It may also be difficult in reality – as we shall see from the empirical evidence contained in this book - to distinguish or at least to disentangle peasant revolt from other forms of rural unrest, and indeed from local and even national politics.

Finally, what Whelpton terms 'crusades' are, he suggests, 'rebellions driven by religion or ideology, ranging from the varieties of liberal and Marxist value-systems behind *sat sal*, the Maoist's People's War, and other, less successful uprisings in recent times, to the Lakhan Thapa revolt against Jang Bahadur analysed in detail by 'Lecomte-Tilouine' (2003)'[3]. We are not comfortable with the term 'crusades', but would argue in any case that the extent to which various rural uprisings had an ideological (as opposed to a practical or pragmatic) objective or mission, remains something to be explored empirically, before they can be classified in a particular way.

Struggles for land rights, for example, are usually not *just* related to 'tensions' or class struggle between the peasantry and landlords, focused on access to land as the means of production – although they may be that. They are often also about rights to land and, beyond that, about a vision of a fairer society – in other words, a political ideology. This point is well made by James C. Scott in his studies of 'everyday forms of peasant resistance' (Scott 1985). Indeed, Whelpton acknowledges that 'one does not have to be a Marxist to acknowledge that ideology generally marches with material interests, so this factor usually operates in tandem with one or more of the other three' (2013: 29). He also comments that it is not always possible to distinguish between political violence and violence applied solely for private gain or straight-forward criminality, and notes that if the distinction were 'hard and fast' there would be no call for what he calls 'an intermediate category' like 'social banditry' – a term coined by Eric Hobsbawm (1959).

As we have already remarked, however, in early state formations, the distinction between those areas where dissidence prevailed and those where the state was nominally at least in control was often unclear, as the 'reach' of the state would wax and wane over time. As a consequence, there were often marginal areas between the areas under control and those beyond the control of the state, where 'dissidence' predominated. It was here,

3. Also discussed elsewhere by Marie Lecomte-Tilouine (Lecomte-Tilouine 2000 and 2013).

pre-eminently, that one found what Hobsbawm identified as 'social bandits'.

Finally, Whelpton usefully draws attention to the fact that not all of these categories involve purely indigenous or local actors but may be affected in various ways by 'external forces'. We shall see in this book that disentangling peasant revolts or uprisings from other forms of rural unrest, rural unrest from other forms of politics, and local struggles from wider national and even international struggles, is no easy matter.

1

The Rise of Gorkha

In the 18th century, population was sparse, with various modes of pre-capitalist production predominating – hunting and gathering from the wild, pastoralism, and shifting agriculture for the most part; settled agriculture, in so far as it existed, was largely reliant on rainfall and irrigation was poorly developed in most of the petty hill states of what would eventually become Nepal (Regmi 1999: 18), and so the agrarian economy was not a reliable basis on which to rely for tax revenues from surplus production. More important for many hill rulers were other resources, including minerals (notably iron and copper) which were exported to India, and control over long distance trade[4], north to Tibet and south to India (ibid pp. 19-20).

It seems that Gorkha was particularly poor, 'being cut off from any direct communication with either the low country (the *terai*) or Tibet, and having no mines, nor other production as basis for commerce' (Regmi 1999: 5). Its expansionist ambitions, however, appear to date back as early as the reign of Narbhupal Shah (1716-1743). An attempt by Gorkha in 1737 to seize the trading centre of Nuwakot (on the borders of the Kathmandu

4. The importance of control over long-distance trade for the maintenance of state power has been noted in a number of cases of early pre-capitalist formations, in Asia and elsewhere (cf Lacoste 1974, Murray 1975, Seddon 1981, Terray 1974).

Valley) from Kathmandu was not successful, but in 1742, Prithvi Narayan Shah became king of Gorkha and resumed the campaign to take Nuwakot and conquer the kingdoms of the Kathmandu Valley. It seems that, in the 1740s, Prithivi Narayan Shah established close relations with Indian arms manufacturers and dealers and brought in technicians to assist with the local production of weapons (Regmi 1999: 6). This, together with the martial qualities of the men of Gorkha, seems to have established a decisive difference between Gorkha and its neighbouring states and helps explain its subsequent rise to power.

Convinced he would not be able to take Kathmandu by force alone, he sought to subdue the Valley by choking its commerce and supply lines. His forces first occupied strategic passes in the surrounding hills, and strangled the vital trade links with Tibet and India. In 1744, he took Nuwakot, which gave him a foothold in Nepal and allowed him to take advantage of the profitable trade that passed through Nuwakot when it came under Gorkha's control. By 1748, Sindhupalchowk and Kabre Palanchowk and other areas immediately to the east of Kathmandu were subjugated, and the passes of Kuti and Kerung, which constituted the main routes through which flowed trade between the Kathmandu Valley and Tibet, also came under Gorkhali control. The conquest of the kingdom of Makwanpur in September 1762 gained the expanding Gorkhali state access to areas of the eastern *terai* through which the kingdoms of the Valley had maintained contact with India.

Resistance in the Kathmandu Valley

The armed forces of the Kathmandu Valley kingdoms which resisted the assault on the Kathmandu Valley by the Gorkhali forces were recruited from many different social groups. It seems they had Khas, Magars, Tamangs from the western hills, and also 'Tirahutiyas' from the *terai*, as well as local Newars in their armies. Jayanta Rana, Parshuram Thapa and his brother Dayaram Thapa were the main commanders of the valley forces. Kirtipur was the town that appears to have put up the greatest resistance to the assault on the Valley by the forces of Prithivi Narayan Shah.

The Gorkhalis had set up a base on Dahachok, a hill on the valley's western rim, from where they mounted their assaults on Kirtipur. They were armed with swords, bows and arrows, and muskets. Resistance, however, was strong; and during the first assault in 1757, the Gorkhali army was badly beaten. As they advanced towards Kirtipur, the Newars went to meet them under the command of Kaji Danuvanta. The two forces fought on the plain of Tyangla Phant to the north-west of Kirtipur. The Newars defended their town ferociously; the Gorkhali commander Kalu Pande was killed, and Prithivi Narayan Shah himself barely escaped with his life, allegedly fleeing into the surrounding hills disguised as a holy man.

Having decided there was little chance of taking Kirtipur by force alone, Shah mounted a blockade in an effort to starve the population into submission. The embargo was enforced by putting to death anybody found on the road with salt or cotton. But the Newars held out. In 1764, Shah ordered his troops to storm the town a second time. This time, the Gorkhalis attacked at night under the command of Shah's brother Suruparatna (or Surpratap). The people of Kirtipur beat off the Gorkhalis again, raining stones on the invaders from the town walls. In the fighting, Surpratap was struck by an arrow in the eye and blinded.

In a bid to cause a famine, Prithivi Narayan Shah now mounted a blockade preventing any grain from passing into the valley. Blockade runners were hanged from the trees on the roads.

The prolonged siege forced the king of Kathmandu to appeal to the British East India Company for help. In August 1767, Captain George Kinloch led a British force towards the valley to rescue its beleaguered inhabitants. He reached to within 75 km of Kathmandu and captured the forts at Sindhuli and Hariharpur; but the Gorkhalis attacked his party on their way and they were forced to retreat to Bettiah. The king of Gorkha now sent his army to attack Kirtipur for a third time, again under the command of his brother, Surpratap.

In response, the three kings of Nepal joined forces and sent their troops to the relief of Kirtipur, but they could not dislodge the Gorkhalis from their positions. A nobleman of Lalitpur named Danuvanta (was this any relation of the commander who had previously led the Kirtipur forces?) crossed over to Shah's side and treacherously let the Gorkhalis into the town. The inhabitants could have fought on, but exhausted by a prolonged siege and assured by Shah's promise of an amnesty, they surrendered. Legend has it, though, that a Newar woman of Kirtipur, called Kirti Laxmi, had fought the invaders disguised as a man named Bhairav Singh. Armed with a bow and arrows, she kept fighting even after the Gorkhalis had taken the town. She was finally captured, however, and kept in captivity, where she took her own life. She is honoured as the heroine of Kirtipur, and is often identified as an avatar of the Holy Goddess Ajimaa of the Newars, who was responsible for saving the kingdom of Kirtipur[5].

Two days later, enraged by the losses inflicted on his army and the injury done to his brother during the protracted war, Shah ordered that the town's prominent inhabitants be killed, and the

---

5. *Kirti Laxmi* (1997), a historical novel by Basu Pasa in Nepal Bhasa, based on 'the true story' of a woman named Kirti Laxmi who fought the Gorkhalis disguised as a man, was published from Kathmandu by Thaunkanhe Prakashan.

noses and lips of everybody cut off. According to historians, the defenders of Kirtipur whose noses were cut off numbered eight hundred and sixty-five. An Italian Capuchin missionary, Father Giuseppe, Prefect of the Roman Mission, wrote that 'it was most shocking to see so many living people with their teeth and noses resembling the skulls of the deceased'. In 1793, when Colonel Kirkpatrick, an envoy of Charles Cornwallis, governor-general of British India, visited Kathmandu 26 years after the battle, he saw these noseless men, and has written about his experience in his memoirs:

"We came to the knowledge of this fact in consequence of observing among the porters who transported our baggage over the hills a remarkable number of noseless men, the singularity of the circumstance leading us to inquire into the cause of it."

His victory in the Battle of Kirtipur was the climax of Prithivi NarayanShah's two-decade-long effort to take possession of the wealthy Kathmandu Valley. After the fall of Kirtipur, he took the other cities relatively easily, Kathmandu and Lalitpur in 1768 and Bhaktapur in 1769, completing his conquest of the valley. He then established the Gorkhali (Shah) dynasty in Nepal by replacing the Mallas.

Resistance in the Eastern Hills

At the time of the rise of Gorkha in the mid -18th century, the Kiranti peoples of the eastern hills enjoyed a high degree of political autonomy, alternating their allegiance between the Malla kings of the Kathmandu Valley and the king of Sikkim. Whelpton devotes several pages to the early 'unification' of Nepal during the late 18th century and discusses both initial resistance to Gorkha expansion and annexation, and also later rebellions against the new Gokhali state, the most persistent of which were in the eastern hills (2013: 29-32).

He agrees that Prithivi Narayan Shah's conquest was facilitated because, as the first hill ruler to import firearms, he had a technical advantage over many adversaries, including the Rais and Limbus of the eastern hills, who still fought with swords and arrows.

During the 1774 campaign in this region, Gorkhali forces were easily able to take the *terai* capitals of the Sen rulers and also to over-run large tracts of hill country, but they then faced seven years of continuing resistance, probably on a guerrilla pattern' (Whelpton 2013: 30).

The Battle of Chainpur, in which the Gorkhali forces were pitted against the armies of Sikkim, took place, for example, in 1776. After its victory there, the Gorkhali state began to consolidate its control of eastern Nepal, in two main phases: firstly, the ethnic groups or 'tribes' of 'near' (*wallo*) and 'middle' (*majh*)[6] Kirant, secondly those of 'further' or 'far' (*pallo)* Kirant, known as Limbuwan (or Limbu territory).

The effective annexation of the eastern hills is attributed by Pradhan (1991) to the willingness of some locals to fight against their own people, to the absence of a united opposition and to the fact that the locals were armed mainly with swords and bows rather than firearms. It does seem highly likely that the expansion of the Gorkhali state was facilitated by its superior military strength, combined with the successful negotiation of strategic alliances: 'the expansion eastwards of the Hindu armies in the 1770s resulted in a series of alliances with potentially troublesome Limbu chiefs flanking them on all sides', based on the promise

6. Today's Bhojpur and Khotang districts were part of *majh* Kirant. Later, the region was known for the purposes of army recruitment as 'east no. 4'. The majority of the population were Rai, but other ethnic groups, including Limbus, Gurungs, Yakkas, Tamangs and Magars, as well as high caste Brahmins and Chhetris and so-called occupational castes or *dalits,* also lived there. Limbus, however, generally tended to live further east, in *pallo* Kirant (Limbuwan).

that the Kirantis would, in return for their support, be granted a measure of internal rule under their own chiefs and guaranteed their rights to 'ancestral lands' (Caplan 1970: 4).

Even so, there was strong resistance, particularly in *pallo* Kirant, where some local Limbu and Sikkimese forces held out until 1786. Fitzpatrick remarks that 'despite partial control of Limbuwan from about 1782, and more substantial control from 1786, political, cultural and economic resistance continued in various forms through to the fall of the Rana regime in 1951, and elements of this resistance could be said to exist still today' (2011: 34)[7]. The political culture of the far eastern hill peoples, who identified themselves as 'Limbu' and their territory as 'Limbuwan', has remained exceptionally strong over the last two centuries. One of the reasons for this relates to their distinctive forms of political and social organization founded on communal forms of land tenure (*kipat*) and a high degree of egalitarianism.

The economic base of local societies in the eastern hills had previously involved a combination of an earlier hunting and gathering economy with pastoralism and 'slash and burn' agriculture, associated with distinctive forms of local community land tenure, rather than individual ownership. While land tenure and land ownership in most of Nepal was organized in the late 18th century around the *raikar* system, in which individuals could effectively hold private title (even if ultimate property rights rested with the state), land in the eastern hills was largely

7. Indeed, as we shall see later, there was significant rural conflict in this region during the 1950s, and later, in part as a result of the growth of 'identity politics' since 1990, and even in the last five years, as the idea of ethnic federalism (led by the Maoists) resulted in a resurgence of political activity in the far eastern hills among ethnic Limbus around the notion of a distinct and potentially autonomous 'Limbuwan' – as indeed did the notion of a distinct state of 'Khumbuwan' in Solu Khumbu.

organized under the *kipat* system, in which land was held communally and individuals had rights and access to it by virtue of their membership of a specific group and through allocation by a local headman or chief.

Waste land and un-cleared forest as well as cultivated land were all considered *kipat* by the locals, whereas, elsewhere in Nepal, various forms of state ownership and individual title predominated. *Kipat* was thus a pre-capitalist form of 'community land tenure' of a kind originally discussed by Karl Marx. Unlike *raikar, kipat* land could, in theory at least, not be sold or given to non-community members. However, prior to 1883, there was no specific restriction on the ability of local communities to give away their *kipat* land, and land thus alienated was often registered as *birta* by those receiving or buying it.

It is not actually clear what control 'pre-unification' chiefs and the rulers of petty states in Kirant, where they existed, had over the allocation of rights to land, or, indeed, whether their powers arose from local circumstances or from recognition by a higher-level ruler (eg the king of Sikkim); but Caplan explains that 'the Shah rulers did not create *subbas* among the Limbus. They only absorbed the traditional headmen into the administrative structure of the new state'.

Caplan remarks that the Limbus of the eastern hills 'did not submit docilely to Gorkhali subjugation and were not hesitant to seek external support for their rebellions against Kathmandu's authority'. During the Nepal-China war of 1788-93, many of them actually joined the enemy. Such rebellions were eventually suppressed, and many Limbus fled their homeland out of fear of reprisals; but the government recognised the need to develop more amicable relations with the Limbus. Accordingly, it proclaimed an amnesty in 1795, 'calling on the fugitive Limbus to return to *pallo kirat* and guaranteeing their traditional customs and privileges' (Regmi 1999: 51) – including, notably their *kipat* collective land-holding rights.

Resistance in the Western Hills

By 1789, resistance to the process of 'unification' had been largely subdued, the *chaubise* and *baise* western hill states had all been annexed and the frontier in the west extended to the Mahakali River (Regmi 1999: 7-8). Once annexed, and reduced in effect to vassal status, these subordinate states initially paid tribute to their overlords, the rulers of the emerging Gorkhali state. Indeed, the political formation that emerged through 'unification' was effectively a tributary state – an amalgamation of subordinate political formations rather than a unified state – and one whose ruling elite was to struggle to retain power well into the 19th century.

In the hills to the immediate west of the Kathmandu Valley, and near to the original petty state of Gorkha, it seems that the Gorkhali state was seen by the locals largely as either a continuation of what they had known previously or as something that brought about minimal change in their immediate circumstances. Many peasants in this region, notably Gurungs and Magars, were recruited from one state into the Gorkhali armies and deployed to support the pacification of others further to the west; the benefits of this were almost certainly significant and generally appreciated by those concerned, even if others may have resented it.

Local rulers were generally brought under Gorkhali jurisdiction and the authority of the emerging Gorkhali state, but as Regmi explains, 'in the western and far-eastern hill areas, Prithivi Narayan Shah generally followed the policy of subjugating principalities without actually annexing their territories' (Regmi

1999: 12). 'As a general rule, the territories of defeated *rajas* were... annexed only when they resisted the Gorkhali invaders to the last, or rebelled after once accepting their suzerainty' (Regmi 1999: 13). This form of indirect rule, enabled the local rulers to maintain their capacity to exploit their own peasantries and thus sustain their position as overlords, despite accepting a degree of political subordination.

Jajarkot was the first principality to accept the status of a vassal under the Gorkhalis in this manner. In a letter to the *raja* of Jajarkot in January 1769, Prithivi Narayan Shah wrote:

'we confirm your ancestral authority within your territory, including your authority to award capital punishment, upgrade or degrade castes, collect levies to finance the sacred thread investiture ceremonies and weddings of royal princes and princesses, and fees for the expiation of caste offences. We also confirm your authority to grant or confiscate *birta* lands and to collect judicial fines, escheats and fees for stamping weights and measures. You shall pay only Rs 701 whenever a new king ascends our throne. When a new king ascends your throne, you shall have authority to collect customary payments from your people'.

This policy, says Regmi, was continued by the successors of Prithivi Narayan Shah when the western and far-western hill areas were subjugated from 1786 to 1789; although circumstances sometimes compelled the Gorkhali rulers to annex territories directly, as when they resisted or rebelled. For example, Kaski, which had initially been given vassal status, was later annexed when the *raja* rebelled – an example of elite politics, one might suggest. Some of the *rajas* displaced by the Gorkhali state were, however, later restored as vassals when this seemed expedient to the Gorkhalis.

The *raja* of Bajura, for example, was granted such status in 1791 in appreciation of the assistance rendered by him during Gorkha's wars with Achham, Doti and Jumla (Regmi 1999: 13). Also, many of those who at first fought against the Gorkhali state, later joined as part of its armed forces against its enemies. For example, Bhakti Thapa, who was later killed while fighting in the Gorkhali army against the English in 1815, had originally been a commander in the army of the *raja* of Lamjung and had been taken prisoner by Gorkha in 1792.

Resistance in the Far West

In the far west, as Whelpton comments, 'Gorkha rule seems to have been felt as more of an alien imposition and particularly strong resistance was encountered in Jumla, which had previously enjoyed a certain primacy among the *baisi* states of the Karnali basin' (2013: 32). At the time of its conquest by Gorkha, Jumla controlled a number of other petty states, including Mustang, which had come under its suzereignty around 1760. The Malla rulers of Jumla were in a position thereby to secure significant revenues both from within their own territory and from other subordinate or vassal states. As early as 1751, a massive sum of Rs 9,000 was raised, through a special levy, to employ labourers, stone-workers, carpenters and architects in the construction of a royal palace, to engage Brahmin priests to perform the appropriate religious ceremonies to sanctify the new buildings, and for the purchase of cloth, cows and other items required for these ceremonies (Regmi 1999: 21).

It seems that, in the Karnali region as a whole, including Jumla, the rights of peasants (*chuni ryots*) on the *raikar* (private) land they cultivated had already developed into a form that permitted transactions in land through the payment of cash; also payment of land taxes to the state were generally in cash. Regmi speculates that 'the fact that most of these areas had once formed part of the Malla Kingdom of Jumla and thus, unlike the other principalities of the (western) hill regions, had been subject to a common polity may have had some bearing on this...' (Regmi 1999: 30). The *chuni ryots* of the Karnali region differed from the majority of the peasants in the western hill states where the term used was generally *mohi,* or tenant farmer. As Regmi remarks, 'the status distinction is obvious enough' – the *chuni ryots* had greater control over their own production and could even raise the money to pay taxes without personally working the land; they were small landowners, whereas the *mohi* was formally a tenant and often a sharecropper.

Jumla was perhaps the most powerful of the *baise* states, and withstood the onslaught of the Gorkhalis for two years before its capital, Chinasim, fell eventually in 1789. Acounts differ as to what then happened to its ruler, Shobhan Shahi; some say he was arrested and brought to Kathmandu, others that he escaped to Mugu, from where he mounted a revolt, which he lost, before mounting another revolt from Humla, which he again lost, before fleeing to Tibet, where he died (Adhikari 1998: 55-59). Jumla was finally pacified in 1793 and it was then governed by a *subba* sent from Kathmandu (Shrestha-Schipper 2013: 260).

Although Jumla thereafter accepted its subordinate status within the Gorkhali state, many Jumlis who were not willing to do so voted with their feet. Whelpton comments that Bishop (1990: 122-146) 'used revenue statistics to calculate that there was a substantial dip in population, which did not return to the pre-conquest level until 1930. Some other principalities in the far west continued to be restive for some time into the 19th century' (Whelpton 2013: 32). By the end of the century, however, the western *chaubisi* and far western *baisi* principalities had all been subjugated or annexed, and the frontier of the Gorkhali state extended to the Mahakali River in the west. Through 1790 and 1791, Kumaon was effectively annexed and Garwhal established a formal relationship with the Gorkhali state whereby the *raja* would pay an annual tribute. It seemed as though the Gorkhali state had effectively subdued all the territories it had 'unified' under its banner.

2

The Expansion and Consolidation of the Gorkhali State

Between 1786 and 1790, Bahadur Shah was able to extend the rule of Kathmandu over the whole territory that is now known as Nepal, adding almost 20,000 square miles to the territories controlled by the House of Gorkha.

Rural Revolt in the Central and Eastern Hills

There remained, however, the potential for rural unrest, even after 'unification'. When, for example, in 1792, Gorkha's expansionism towards the north and its aggressive policy towards Tibet led to the intervention of the Chinese army, the Chinese called on the relatively newly subjugated peoples of the central and eastern hills to join them, and to rise up in revolt against their new masters. It is not clear to what extent they were calling on local rulers and tribal chiefs, or on the mass of the peasantry, to rise in revolt; but not only the Limbus but also the Tamangs did indeed rise up, largely for what might be termed political reasons, effectively refusing to accept the authority of the Gorkhali state.

The Gorkhali state responded to the revolt of the Tamangs rapidly and brutally. Whelpton (2013: 31) cites a royal order of 1793 issued with reference to the Tamangs of the 1,500 rivers region, in what are today Rasuwa and Nagarkot:

When people belonging to the Murmi (Tamang) community engaged in rebellion (*kul*)[8], they were captured and beheaded. If any of the rebels is hiding there, seize him and hand him over to our *amali* (government official or judge). If it has been proved that you were not involved in the rebellion, no action will be taken against those who were not so involved (from Regmi 1984: 129, quoted in Holmberg 2006: 36)

Whelpton comments that 'repression was the immediate response in Limbuwan as well, but the government in Kathmandu later adopted a more conciliatory policy, promising amnesty to those who had taken part in the rebellion if they returned to their former homes' (2013: 31). The difference between the treatment of the Tamang rebels and that of the Limbus is striking. Whelpton comments, tellingly, as regards the latter, that 'the key problem was that with the low population density in Nepal at this time, it was difficult to replace cultivators who fled to another territory, and this meant loss of revenue for the central government' (Ibid).

Indeed, one of the major policies of the Gorkhali state at the end of the 19th century, was to encourage immigration, land clearance, settlement and cultivation so as to maximize revenues from those occupying the land, for the pacification and administration of yet new territories, thereby establishing a positive feedback system leading to further expansion. This meant that, in reality, a combination of 'stick and carrot' was adopted for many decades, in order to create a viable and prosperous economy and society. Where the rural population was settled and within 'reach', the state was able to maintain effective control; further afield, and particularly where land was in plentiful supply and the local farming population sparse, immigrants who came as

8. The translation of *kul* here as 'rebellion' clearly makes sense, but it normally refers to a clan or family, or to 'all' or 'the totality', and so it is not entirely clear what was meant precisely.

cultivators were generally welcomed and given concessions; only when established were they taxed.

Taxation at the local level could be onerous, and the state was concerned that over-taxation should not jeopardize the overall objective of raising revenue and, recognizing that this depended upon encouraging forest clearance, settlement and cultivation above all, was careful to maintain 'reasonable' levels of demand for taxation and unpaid additional services. M. C. Regmi quotes an order, issued in 1790, which stated that 'peasants are being greatly harassed by the imposition of compulsory and unpaid services ... so that they cannot even cultivate their lands properly. Accordingly, from 1790 we exempt them from porterage and other services ... No civil or military official shall exact such services ... except on fair wages' (Regmi, M.C. 1964, *Land Tenure*, iii, 57-58).

The state was always, even in later periods under the Ranas, very cautious about over-taxing the peasantry, particularly in sparsely populated and remote areas. The effective combination of the 'stick and the carrot' may explain the apparent relative lack of peasant resistance, unrest and revolt, throughout the 19th century, to which Jang Bahadur Rana referred. But we shall return to this issue later.

Expansion and Resistance in the Far West

In the far west, Bahadur Shah was able to conquer first Jumla and then Acham, Bjhang and Doti and to reach the Mahakali River. In the west, through 1790 and 1791, Kumaon was effectively annexed and Garwhal established a formal relationship with the Gorkhali state whereby the *raja* agreed to pay an annual tribute. This might have been the point at which to halt the westwards expansion, but the Gorkhali army had gained momentum and to the west lay Kumaon and Garhwal and the minor states beyond.

It was, as Ludwig Stiller (2017: 185) remarks, an opportunity to tempting to resist.

Bahadur Shah was temporarily obliged to turn his attention to the north, in order to respond to the Chinese invasion of Nepal, which resulted in the Nepal-China war of 1792, and to the visit of Captain Kirkpatrick as an emissary from the British East India Company, which had offered to mediate in the conflict. In 1794, however, the young King Rana Bahadur came of age and shortly afterwards took control, eventually, in 1797, having Bahadur Shah arrested and imprisoned. From 1794 to 1804, there was no further systematic effort on the part of Kathmandu to continue with the westward expansion of the Gorkhali state. But in 1795, an attempt was made by the local Gorkhali *sardar* (commander) to extend control over a part of the Kumaon *terai*, which belonged to the Nawab of Avadh (Oudh)[9], even though this was against Kathmandu's policy of avoiding any attacks on territories under the Nawab's authority.

The Nawab began military preparations and the *sardar* was instructed by Kathmandu to take his troops out of the area at once. In February the same year, Garwhal pleaded with Kathmandu for a remission of the annual tribute and so, concerned that Garwhal might ally itself with the Nawab and with the British, Kathmandu agreed to reduce the amount involved. But a few years later, in 1804, largely owing to the initiatives of its commanders, the Gorkhali army crossed the Pindar River and engaged with the largely mercenary force of the Garhwalis in series of battles in which the latter were decisively beaten and Garhwal was obliged to accept Gorkhali rule.

9. After the Mughal Empire was established, some of the rulers of the petty hill states of what is now Nepal acknowledged the Mughal emperor or local Nawabs as their ultimate overlord and thereby gained legitimacy for the territories they commanded in the *terai*.

The Limits to Expansion

The Gorkhali forces went on to achieve military victories in the petty states of the Barha and Athara Thakurai against troops deployed by Hindoor and Nadun, with the help of Sirmoor, and then to cross the Sutlej River and press on for Kangra, a formidable stronghold to the west of the Beas River and effectively the gateway to Kashmir. Here, however, they experienced a serious set-back when the Sikh army under Ranjit Singh arrived in June 1809 to support Sansur Chand of Nadun and to oppose the Gorkhali expansion. Ranjit Singh had signed a treaty with the British in April, but after a stand-off between the forces of the Gorkhali and the Sikh states, following which a truce and a treaty were agreed and the Gorkhalis withdrew his troops to the east of the Sutlej River, he was prepared to consider a deal with the Gorkhali state. This was not to be.

The Gorkhali forces now returned to attack Sirmoor and Hindoor, both of which fell to the Gorkhalis, rapidly followed in 1810 by Joobul, Poodur and Bussahir. By 1810-11, however, tensions were rising all along the southern border of the Gorkhali state between it and the British East India Company, which was also in an expansionist phase. The British had made it clear that while they would not interfere in the plans of the Gorkhali state to expand to the west in the hills, they would not tolerate expansion 'below the hills' - this message, expressing the British 'principle of limitation', was communicated to the Gorkhalis by Colonel Ochterlony in a letter sent in April 1810.

But whereas the British based their notion of jurisdiction on geographical location, the Gorkhali state defined their possessions by political subordination. As Stiller comments: 'they felt that if they bought a *raja,* no matter how petty or how large, under their rule, they were entitled to the total possessions of that *raja,* whether they be in the hills or the plains' (Stiller

2017: 241). These possessions, crucially, included the natural and human resources of the territories under their jurisdiction, and the taxes and tribute that accrued as a result. Indeed, one might best characterize the Gorkhali state in the early decades of the 19th century as 'a tributary state'[10].

The state accrued wealth essentially through its power, authority and jurisdiction over other subordinate states, which had vassal status and gave 'tribute' to Gorkha, and also increasingly by its own control over an increasing number of trade routes, from which it derived revenues, over the natural resources of the forests and, increasingly importantly, over an expanding cultivated area of settled farmers and peasants, from whom it extracted surplus in the form of rent and or tax. This could be referred to as a form of what Marx termed 'the Asiatic mode of production'.

Rural Unrest in the Gorkhali state

Whelpton suggests that 'once the turmoil of 'unification' and its immediate aftermath was over, from the beginning of the 19th century, the mass of the population did, by and large remain in the state of passive obedience, which Jang Bahadur described to Orfeur Caveagh' (2013: 38). He then suggests, vaguely, and without specific references, that 'there must have inevitably have been small scale instances of rebellion at village level and at least in some areas, the possibility of a serious outburst does seem to have influenced government policy' (sic). He does not, however, identify any examples of these possible 'instances of rebellion at village level', or indeed refer to any other instance of peasant revolt until a rebellion in Gorkha in the 1870s, led by a local Magar leader who claimed to be a reincarnation of the saint Lakhan Thapa.

One explanation for this may simply be that the evidence

10. See Terray (1974) for an African case study; also Lacoste (1974) for a case study in the Maghreb.

of peasant unrest in the immediate 'post-unification' period has not been examined in sufficient detail; another may be that there were, in fact, relatively few instances of rural revolt or rebellion. If the latter is the case, then it may be related, as we have already argued, to the fact that, although during this early period the expanded Gorkhali state was concerned to increase the revenues accruing to the state, the sparseness of the population meant that the priority in agriculture was to encourage immigration, land clearance and cultivation, with a view to raising revenues largely by extending the area under cultivation rather than by raising the level of taxes.

Under such circumstances, when the extension of cultivation rather than increasing the level of taxation was the preferred option (and the dominant mode of production at the local level was in any case one of extensive or shifting cultivation combined with livestock production and the exploitation of 'wild' resources), the locals could often move out of range of state tax administration and collection. It is also possible that, particularly in areas where they were incomers rather than long-established groups, as was the case in some hill areas and more generally in the *terai,* they were not politically organized and had only 'the weapons of the weak' with which to respond to over-burdensome taxation by the state – ie running away rather than resisting.

As the population increased, however, and settled farming began to become the dominant mode of production, this form of tax avoidance became increasingly difficult, the level of taxes increased, and it seems that for a time at least the exploitation of the peasantry increased. The confiscation of *birta* land from *birta* holders, for example, which began to gain momentum during the first decade of the 19th century and was implemented with a view to extending state control over newly reclaimed land for revenue purposes – often, it appears, resulted in resistance and rural unrest. The confiscation and conversion of *birta* and other land 'had a far-reaching impact on the status and condition of the cultivating class' – including the peasantry: 'such conversion did not necessarily lead to the eviction of existing occupants, but they were reduced to the status of tenants on the land which they had previously cultivated on free-hold tenure' (Regmi 1999: 75).

Many former independent peasants found themselves obliged to pay rent, usually under the *adhiya* (half and half) system, on the land they cultivated, and their incomes tended to fall accordingly. The response was often, initially, a complaint to the authorities; if and when this proved futile, it often resulted in the abandonment of farm and field, and emigration from the locality, so that some areas became de-populated; but 'the protest of the dispossessed *birta* owners to the 1805 confiscation measures did not long remain passive. Particularly in Tanahu and other areas in the western hill region violent clashes broke out between them and the government officials deputed to administer the measures. The government understandably adopted a strong attitude towards such opposition. The ringleaders were arrested and brought to Kathmandu in chains' (Regmi 1999: 77, cited in Basnet 2008: 20).

Officials sent to confiscate *birta* lands in Syangja district were directed to arrest and put in chains the Brahmins of Karkineta, who had promised to surrender their wives, their names, their lands and their lives all at the same time, and had gone into hiding. The officials were informed that if any Brahmins were to be killed in the course of this action, they (the officials) would not be held to account. Despite or arguably because of this, the protest organized by the Brahmin *birta* owners in the western hill regions became so acute in late 1805 that the government even banned their entry into Kathmandu without passports (Regmi 1999: 77).

There were further changes to the system of rural administration in the second decade of the 19th century. In 1812, the *adhiya* system was finally discarded as the basis for rent assessment in favour of the *kut* system (of fixed rents) in the Kathmandu Valley and large parts of the hill regions; in 1816, the system was further clarified. The level of *kut* rents was usually, however, higher than that of *adhiya,* and if output was lower than usual in a particular season, the peasant was still obliged to pay the same fixed rent. Furthermore, peasants could be evicted if they did not pay; although there is contradictory evidence in this respect (cf Regmi 1999: 89-92). This created new difficulties, and contributed to a process of what might be termed class formation. *Kut* land grants were sometimes made to intermediaries rather than to actual cultivators, giving them effective jurisdiction over the peasantry and encouraging what Regmi significantly terms 'sub-infeudation'.

Regmi states that 'the evidence is thus clear that the condition of the peasantry deteriorated to a considerable extent during the period after the political unification of Nepal' (1999: 99), although it is likely that the extent to which this change occurred varied considerably from place to place. One consequence was an increase in the number of cultivators leaving their holdings; another was the occasional localized outbreak of peasant revolt. Regmi notes that, 'the government attempted to mitigate their difficulties by controlling the rates of payments collected from them and giving them a measure of tenurial security'; but, even accepting this rather benign interpretation of the measures adopted by government, it was also the case that 'rent and tenancy legislation intended to benefit the peasantry is always difficult to enforce, particularly in a situation where there is a close conformity of association and interest among revenue officials, *birta* owners and *jagidars* and the more powerful elements in the village'[11].

In addition to the burden of taxation and rent, peasants were also subject to demands for 'obligatory services' (*jhara*) of various kinds, although Regmi considers that 'the Gorkhali rulers appear to have tried from the very beginning to insure that the growing burden of *jhara* services did not alienate the peasantry', and refers to several measures intended to mitigate or compensate for such demands (Regmi 1999: 113-116). He notes, significantly, that such measures were applied mainly 'in areas which were sparsely populated or inhabited by unruly communities, and were situated close to the borders' – that is, where there was the greatest risk that demands for *jhara* services on top of everything else would result in peasants simply abandoning their fields and migrating elsewhere, or by revolting and threatening security.

He suggests, for example, that 'it can hardly be a coincidence that areas between the Koshi and the Tista Rivers (where compensation for *jhara* labour was provided) were inhabited by the Limbu and other Kirati communities who had not yet fully accepted subjugation by Gorkha (Regmi 1999: 116). So, it seems that rebellions did occur from time to time in different parts of the country against the Gorkhali regime in the immediate 'post-unification' period. In some instances, usually where the local population was settled and within the effective 'reach' of the state (as in the western hills), they were put down with considerable brutality. In his discussion of slavery in the post-unification Gorkhali state: 'rebels were lucky if they were enslaved, for capital punishment was usually awarded to all those who were above the age of 12 years'.

11. Regmi himself admits that 'at the same time, one would suspect that the measures undertaken by the government from time to time 'for the benefit of the peasantry' were not always meant to be actually enforced' (Regmi 1999: 99-100).

3

The Post-War Gorkhali State

The ambitions of the Gorkhali state and the British East India Company - were effectively in contradiction with each other, and relations between the two gradually deteriorated. Eventually, this brought to an end the westwards expansion of the Gorkhali state and led inexorably, in 1814, to conflict and the Anglo-Nepali War of 1814-1816.

In 1816, after a two-season war with the British East India Company, the Gorkhalis were forced to accept defeat, and reluctantly ceded many of their territorial gains in the far western *terai,* including those in the newly acquired regions (*naya muluk*), to the Company, in the Treaty of Sugauli. The British then gave the territory to the kingdom of Awadh, whose Muslim nawab and court were famous for their profligate lifestyle in Lucknow. The nawab had lent the Company funds to finance their campaign against the Gorkhalis, and the British saw him as a useful ally to buffer the hostile Sikh and Maratha states nearby. The territory was ruled by the king of Tulsipur, a tributary state of Awadh, for the next four decades.

After the war, the situation that had generated the disputes over jurisdiction and authority in the border regions that had led to open conflict, had to be regularized and overhauled, and the border between India and Nepal finally demarcated and agreed. There was also now an impetus to reform aspects of the

Gorkhali state, notably the system of local administration and tax collection, with the main objective of ensuring a stable basis for increasing revenue for the government.

The Consolidation of the Gorkhali state

In the hill regions, including the Kathmandu Valley, experiments undertaken between 1820 and 1827 included both arrangements ('settlements') with individual *ryots* and also with village headmen for the entire village as a unit. In 1828, the appointment of local revenue functionaries on a five year basis was tried in the eastern *terai* and then continued in 1834 for another five year term. In 1838, revenue functionaries in the western *terai* were appointed on the same basis. All of this suggests a process of further development in the administration of the Asiatic mode of production by the Gorkhali state.

The general trend as a result of all this was an upwards movement in rents, which tended to disadvantage the peasantry, combined with a gradual shift from in-kind payments to payments in cash, which suited all parties, but forced peasants increasingly to sell at least some of their output to meet their fiscal obligations even as the government was attempting to fix the price of rice and other agricultural commodities, 'mainly with the objective of lowering the costs of feeding the army' and, more generally, maintaining the growing bureaucracy (Regmi 1999: 179-185). The level of rents determined in the course of the 1837 rent settlement appears to have been the highest ever in the history of Nepal – in the hills and in the *terai* (Regmi 1999: 185).

Those who were unable to meet the tax requirements were in trouble. Some were evicted; others chose to abandon their fields and emigrate[12]. Regmi suggests that 'the post-war period in fact,

12. Regmi notes that 'Pallokirat was one of the areas worst affected by the problems of indebtedness and emigration' (Regmi 1999: 194, note 163).

witnessed a large-scale exodus of people from several parts of Nepal to Indian territory' (Regmi 1999: 194). Local people also complained and, in some cases apparently, revolted – although we have little detail of rural unrest at this period. During the 1830s, the government was compelled in some instances to re-think its policy; but overall it stuck to its guns - literally. Payment was often obtained by the use of force and, if necessary the army was deployed.

On the other hand, those who managed to make their payments and maintain cultivation were rewarded with more secure land occupancy rights (Regmi 1999: 185-86). Also, *jhara* (forced labour) for various services declined and there was a trend – which had begun as early as 1790 (Regmi 1964: iii 57-58, cited above) - towards payment for portering and other labour previously provided by locals 'for free'. At the same time, during the late 1820s and the 1830s, measures were taken to improve the condition of slaves and bondsmen, in part to attract back those who had fled punitive taxation and rents, or escaped from slavery and/or bondage to India, to return and reclaim waste land for settlement (Regmi 1999: 189-191). This suggests an early stage in the progressive transformation of the Asiatic mode of production into something different, which would be increasingly based on the reality of 'private' land ownership.

It was still government policy that land was to be reclaimed and arable land used primarily for subsistence by peasant farmers. Still, the government did not officially permit rent-receiving land ownership, except through *birta* grants or *jagir* assignments. This, it could be argued, suggests the continuation in broad terms of the Asiatic mode of production. In reality, however, the situation at the local level was complex, and the simplistic notion of 'the state' directly confronting and exploiting 'the peasantry' somewhat misleading. Throughout this period, and indeed even in the previous period of 'unification' to some extent, cultivators could be owners, tenants or sharecroppers, and there was a plethora of intermediaries, some locals and some officials, between 'the state' and 'the peasantry'. Local intermediaries included those *chuni ryots* who possessed such extensive landholdings with jurisdiction over the lands occupied by others, including often entire villages, that they were called *zamindars* (Regmi 1999: 32 note 80).

This was a category of state official originally introduced in 1793 to reform tenurial conditions in both the *terai* and the hill regions, following reforms undertaken in early that year by the British East India Company. There were large numbers of *zamindars* in both the eastern and western *terai*, and also in some parts of the Karnali region; they paid land taxes to the state but their land was cultivated by sharecroppers (Regmi 1999: 32-33). Even so, Regmi emphasizes, importantly, that 'while *zamindars* in India became proprietors of the land, their counterparts in Nepal remained nothing more than revenue collection functionaries' (Regmi 1999: 93). By this time, however, even if formally they were not private landowners, they were, in effect landlords, extracting surplus from the peasantry under their jurisdiction in the form of rent, and paying themselves taxes to the state.

In the far western hills of the Karnali region, where land taxes were generally paid in cash, *jagirdars* were initially appointed and paid salaries in cash to oversee the collection of taxes by the commander of the local military unit; but from 1805 onwards, lands were actually assigned to them as *jagir*, with jurisdiction to collect taxes/rents directly themselves from the peasantry, or (in some cases) from a 'sub-tenant' – leading to what Regmi (significantly) calls 'sub-infeudation'[13].

13. Peasants cultivating *jagir* lands under conditions of 'sub-infeudation' occupied more or less the same position as those cultivating *birta* and *guthi* lands; Regmi remarks that 'they rarely find a place in the revenue literature of this period, except in so far as they were considered a part of the general mass of the peasantry' (1999: 97).

In the central and eastern hills, by contrast, this level of authority was matched only by the headmen of *kipat*-owning Kirat communities, which resembled those formations described variously by Marx in the *Grundrisse* as 'tribal' and 'Germanic'. In the western hills also, it is possible that, despite the prevalence of peasant communities and virtual absence of *zamindars*, village headmen exercised a somewhat similar, though probably more constrained, authority over local villagers. Indeed, Regmi discusses the range of 'levies' collected by village headmen in the hill regions for various purposes (Regmi 1999: 66). The same may well have been the case in parts of the *terai* where local Tharu chiefs were given responsibilities by the state to raise taxes from local villagers.

Some of the indigenous (*adhivasi*) modes of production remained relatively 'primitive' in terms of their technology, largely involving fishing, hunting and gathering; others were more developed and included shifting cultivation and livestock production; yet others were involved in more or less settled cereal agriculture. Some remained, in socio-political terms, at the level of 'communities' or 'bands'; others had a more complex structure and were organized in clans and/or tribal groups, sometimes with village elders and/or clan heads; yet others were more hierarchical and had tribal chiefs and rulers, and identified themselves as 'ethnic groups'. It is clear, therefore, that at the local level there were still various different 'modes of production' in operation, which, while embedded within a wider political economy, nevertheless had their own dynamic, and also had implications for the operation and development of that wider political economy.

Whatever their mode of production, and their social and political characteristics, in so far as they were for the most part cultivators subordinate to the Gorkhali state, most of the population could be broadly characterized as peasants (in Wolf's terms), subject to state jurisdiction and authority, and obliged to pay rent and taxes. The Gorkhali state had already, by the end of the first few decades of the 19th century, evolved into a powerful apparatus, presiding over an assemblage of social formations, characterized by its overall capacity to control and coerce, if needs be, and to raise revenues. This was not a feudal state, but rather what Marx referred to (inadequately) as an 'Oriental state' with an 'Asiatic mode of production'. This was to be consolidated under the Ranas, progressively, into a distinctive form of 'prebendalism'[14]

---

14. Prebendalism refers to political systems where state officials (civil and military) feel they have a right to a share of government revenues, and use them to benefit their own extended families and social networks. See Gallissot for a discussion in relation to pre-colonial Algeria.

4

The Regime of Jung Bahadur Rana

Regmi comments that 'the emergence of Rana rule marks a turning point in the history of Nepal. To be sure, this event per se did not herald an era of change. It would not even be correct to say that the Rana's economic policies and programmes marked a radical departure from those followed by their predecessors. Rather, that Rana take-over of power synchronized with a number of internal and external developments which made it possible for the Rana rulers to adjust their economic policies and programmes in a more effective manner than their predecessors' (Regmi 1988: 3).

The external developments could be summarized as the settlement achieved with the British in the three decades after the Anglo-Nepali war (1814-1816), whereby the territory of we can now call the state of Nepal was more clearly defined and delimited, and the Ranas were assured – and took measures themselves to assure – that their rule over this territory would not be contested, at least by the British; but were obliged to accept a British representative (a Resident) in the capital. Nepal became 'a semi-colonial state' – a term used by Lenin and Mao Tse Tung to describe states that in the late nineteenth and early twentieth centuries were penetrated by imperial capital, trade, and political influence, but which preserved their juridical and formal political independence[15].

As regards internal developments, Regmi suggests that 'the (domestic) history of Rana rule in Nepal is basically an account of how an impoverished family, which nevertheless ranked high in the social and political scale, and belonged to Gorkha's traditional military aristocracy, was able to grab political power and use that power to build up a centralized state and administration' (1988: 5). He argues that 'the government, under the Rana political system, merely functioned as an instrument to carry out the personal wishes and interests of the ruling Rana Prime Minister, and its main domestic pre-occupation was the exploitation of the country's resources in order to enhance the personal wealth of the Rana ruler and his family' (1988: 6).

He explicitly contrasts this with that prevailing in pre-industrial England, where landed property was the foundation of political authority and where, even at the beginning of the 19th century, Britain was still ruled by landowners (1988: 6). The term 'feudalism' is, therefore inappropriate, as a characterization of the political economy of Nepal under the Ranas, at least as far as Regmi is concerned. On the other hand, he suggests that 'the functions of both revenue collection and civil administration largely belonged to the landowning elites' (1988: 19)[16]. The development of the administration of rural areas and of the army were both features of the early Rana period, leading the consolidation of control over the rural areas by a bureaucratic state, serving the interests of

15. Other examples include Persia, China, Thailand, Afghanistan, Yemen, and Ethiopia.
16. I would prefer to refer to these state functionaries as 'land lords', rather than as 'land owners' (which, by and large, they were not) as their ability to extract surplus from the local peasantry in the form of rent was by virtue of their appointment and/or recognition by the state.

a ruling elite – a form of prebendalism, or what some have called 'command feudalism'[17].

The 19th century Nepali state paid emoluments to its employees and functionaries partly or wholly through assignments of taxable lands and villages rather than through payments of money; such assignments were known as *jagir*. The system was used on such a wide scale that legislation banning the payment of cash salaries to government employees so long as taxable lands were available for assignment as *jagir* remained on the statute book throughout the period of Rana rule, albeit with varying degrees of effectiveness (Regmi 1988: 29-30). In addition, there were four main categories of what Regmi calls 'infra-state agencies' responsible for revenue collection: *rajya, birta, guthi* and *kipat.*

Rajas of vassal principalities were also entitled to collect and appropriate revenues from the territories under their jurisdiction; these included Bajura, Bajhang and Jajarkot in the far west and Mustang in the north-west. *Guthi* were grants made to monasteries and temples, or to other religious or charitable associations. *Kipat* was a system confined to the Kirat ethnic groups, notably the Limbus of the far eastern hills. The *birta* system was different; under this system, arable land, forest, and villages were granted to individuals on a tax-free basis, enabling them to appropriate surpluses directly themselves; this system, then, allowed for the development of land 'owners', as well as land lords.

---

17. Gallissot uses these terms to describe pre-colonial Algeria. He argues that 'although the fiscal character of exploitation on the one hand, and the public and military nature of the social category at the head of the hierarchy on the other, give as Asiatic aspect to the society', the level of development of the productive forces and the class structure suggest that 'pre-colonial Algerian society is truly feudal, distinguished only by one singularity: the primarily fiscal character of the oppression' (Gallissot 1975: 438)

Less than three months after Jung Bahadur Rana became prime minister, he made arrangements to compensate former *birta* holders for the *birta* land confiscated in 1805-06. But few, apart from the Ranas themselves, were able to take advantage of this arrangement - and it was not until 1882 that Ranoddip Simha Rana took effective measures to compensate other *birta* holders through allotments of taxable *jagir* land. *Jagirs* absorbed a sizeable proportion of revenues, but the Ranas appropriated the lion's share of *jagir* incomes to themselves; and the largest beneficiary was the prime minister himself. This is a classic characteristic of 'prebendalism'.

In addition to these various mechanisms for raising state levies, were Crown levies, which accrued specifically to the royal household and the palace. The monarchy was retained, but was marginal in most respects to the political economy of Nepal, serving a largely legitimizing and religious role. Nepal under the Ranas was effectively ruled not by the Shah royal family but by a family dynasty of hereditary prime ministers.

Suggestions that the political economy of Nepal under this regime was 'stagnant' in any way are misplaced and mistaken. This was no static and unchanging Asiatic mode of production or 'Oriental Despotism' of the kind identified by Marx and Lenin or Wittfogel (1957); it was an authoritarian but effective regime with a state apparatus (army and administration) committed to increasing revenues for the ruling class as a whole and particularly for the ever-expanding Rana family, associated with a growing and relatively dynamic agrarian economy, which benefited from its relationship with British India by exporting agricultural and forest-derived raw materials (mainly from the *terai*) and importing manufactured and luxury goods on an increasing scale.

5

The Consolidation of the Rana Regime

State revenues rose between 1851 and 1861 from around NRs 1.4 million to NRs 3.5 million or two and a half times more than previously; in 1877, the last year of Jung Bahadur's regime, it was estimated by Daniel Wright that the total revenue of Nepal was about NRs 9.6 million. Nearly ten years later, G. H. D. Gimlette felt that NRs 10 million was 'nearer the mark' (cited in Blaikie, Cameron & Seddon 1980). Even taking inflation into consideration, this was a substantial increase in real terms. One explanation was that government policies and incentives to promote immigration, land clearance, settlement and cultivation were by and large successful, and the area under cultivation available for taxation increased. A second is that the efficiency in the process of administration and tax collection increased significantly as the Rana regime became increasingly bureaucratic and the army was deployed effectively to maintain overall control. A third is that revenues were increased as a result of the export of timber and other forest products on an increasing scale as demand grew in India.

In fact, the evidence suggests that all three of these provide elements of an explanation. As far as the first is concerned, Regmi remarks that 'thanks largely to immigration from India, the cultivated area in the *terai* region increased steeply during the half-century of Rana rule. The trend inevitably had a positive impact on the role of that region as the major source of state revenues' (1988: 114). As for the second, Regmi provides ample evidence that the early Ranas built the foundations for an effective system of fiscal administration, particularly in the *terai,* that lasted 'for well over a century until the 1960s' (1988: 77).

This included the appointment of *jimidars* (a new category of revenue functionary) for each *mauja* (the basic administrative unit below the district) and an increase in the number of army battalions responsible for supporting the fiscal administration. Regmi concludes that the system of *jimidars* operating at the level of the *mauja* and the 'the establishment of a permanent revenue collection office at the district level was the most important Rana contribution' (1988: 90) to fiscal administration. The bulk of revenues so collected were from the *terai,* and particularly from the eastern *terai,* which contributed nearly three out of every four rupees (Regmi 1988: 93).

A fourth factor in the equation is that it seems that, at least in some instances and in some areas, the level of taxes on the peasantry increased in real terms. The response of the peasantry to the tax burden imposed upon them was manifold but does not appear to have often involved outright revolt or rural unrest. At first, it appears, they tended to appeal against increases, when and where they were introduced. Often, it seems moreover, the state was willing to heed their concerns, and respond to them. Regmi insists that 'the Ranas appear to have followed a very circumspect policy in the field of agrarian taxation. Their primary concern was not to increase the volume of agrarian tax revenues but to ensure that it did not fall below current levels' (1988: 118-119); in quite a few cases there is evidence that the regime was open to the concerns of the local peasantry as regards tax increases.

For example, Bir Shumshere appears to have raised agrarian tax rates in the western *terai* region only once during his fifteen year rule; the increase, approved in 1892, amounted to 2 paisa in the *rupee*, or just over 3 per cent (Regmi 1988: 119). It is my view that the regime *was* concerned to increase total revenues; but wherever possible by the old policy of promoting the extension of cultivation, mainly in the *terai* and mainly by importing capital and labour from India – in other words, promoting development by an investment in capital, land and labour, rather than by squeezing the peasantry. Indeed, Regmi effectively accepts this argument in his concluding discussion (Regmi 1988: 263).

On the other hand, it remained the case that when tax increases became too onerous, particularly where there was little scope for further extension of the area under cultivation, the response by the peasantry was emigration. The evidence strongly suggests that, towards the end of the 19th century, as the limits to the extension of cultivation were reached, and population density began to increase, particularly in the hill regions, migration became an increasingly common response to growing taxation and indebtedness, as it was to be during the 20th century.

There is little evidence of peasant unrest in the *terai* during the Rana period, largely it seems for these two reasons. Firstly, the state was cautious in increasing taxes to the point where there was a risk of rural unrest; and secondly, perhaps, because of the 'safety-valve' provided by an open frontier with British India to the south. There were, however, some signs of dissidence in both the western and the eastern hills; these, though, took the form of elite politics and local rebellion against the regime, or of individual dissenters, rather than of peasant unrest.

The Revolt of Lakhan Thapa Magar

The revolt of Lakhan Thapa Magar in the 1870s has been examined in some detail by Marie Lecomte-Tilouine (2000, 2003). Whelpton confines himself to a terse passing comment: 'this was a messianic revolt in which a subordinated group saw a chance of turning the tables on its overlords with divine assistance, but it did not take hold on a large scale and his (Lakhan's) house was swiftly surrounded by government troops, and Lakhan Thapa himself was hanged' (2013: 39). There is quite a lot more to this revolt, however, than that short summary suggests.

Lakhan Thapa was probably born in 1834. In 1854, at the age of 20, he joined the Magar battalion (Purano Gorkha Gana) of the Nepalese Army. Not long after this, on 2 June 1857, a Gurung *jamadar* had been sentenced to death for being involved in a conspiracy to assassinate Jung Bahadur, and the government planned to turn the guns on some 1700-1800 of his colleagues if they did not go ahead with the execution. Luckily, according to one account (cf Hasrat 1971: 334, cited in Lecomte-Tilouine 2000: 79), the British Resident, George Ramsay, was able to persuade the minister in charge to change his plans and a potential bloodbath – and possibly a rebellion - was averted[18].

One month later, in July 1857, Lakhan Thapa's battalion was deployed to Lucknow, along with 24 others, all led by Jang Bahadur Rana himself, to aid the British at the time of the 'Great Mutiny'. According to the British Resident, George Ramsay, 'from the moment he reached Gorakhpur, on his march towards Lucknow, Maharaja Jung Bahadur, by his own account, was in communication with the rebel leaders, who offered to make him king of Lucknow if he would join their cause and turn upon the British army. This had an ill-effect upon the Gorkha soldiery, many of whom openly gave out that they would return to the plain during the next cold season to annex certain of our districts' (Hasrat 1971: 336). Lecomte-Tilouine suggests that 'Lakhan

18. According to a letter written by the same Resident, quoted by Whelpton (1991: 211), the Gurung *jamadar* was put to death by his own regiment at the Tundikhel, as ordered by the government (Lecomte-Tilouine 2000: 79 footnote 10),

Thapa was among those Nepalese troops who were in contact with these rebels and perhaps found in them a model for his own programme' (2000: 83).

In any case, Lakhan Thapa quit the army in 1869 after reaching the rank of captain, and returned to his home village of Bungkot, in the neighbourhood of Manakamana's temple, in Gorkha District. There he gradually established himself as a local ruler, accumulating sufficient wealth to build a palace, a fort and an exercise ground for his soldiers. In 1871, he was consecrated as a local king or *raja* by the people of the region. His association with the worship of Sri Manakamana was also part of his evident charisma; indeed, he actually established a temple dedicated to Manakamana inside the fort and claimed to be the reincarnation or avatar of the saint Lakhan Thapa, whose importance in the history of the rise of Gorkha is emphasized and detailed by Lecomte-Tilouine (2000: 84-87).

In 1874, he began to mobilize opposition to the regime of Jung Bahadur and in 1876 he launched a rebellion from Bungkot against Jung Bahadur Rana and his regime. The biography of Jung Bahadur Rana, written by his son, reports that, at this time, 'a rebellion of a somewhat curious nature disturbed the peace of the country. A certain Gorkha, formerly a soldier in the army, set himself up as a king...' (Rana 1974: 302, cited in Lecomte-Tilouine 2000: 82). The same source notes that 'his graceful manners and persuasive tone soon procured him an armed following of 1,500 men, at the head of whom he threatened to march to the capital, and after assassinating Jung Bahadur, to seize the reins of government, and inaugurate the golden age of Nepalese history' (Rana 1974, cited in Lecomte-Tilouine 2000: 87). Another source, Pramode Shamshere Rana, suggests that 'his preaching attracted a sizeable following for his mission to overthrow the Rana rule. About two thousand young men rallied behind him and he managed also to get (hold) of some small arms' (Rana 2000: 49).

As the movement grew, Jang Bahadur Rana came to know of it and sent the Devi Dutt regiment to Gorkha to suppress the rebellion. As his son describes it in his biography of Jung Bahadur Rana, 'on receiving news of this insurrection, the Maharaja at once despatched a few companies of the Devi Dutt regiment to put down the fanatic, instructing them not to use force unless they were met with force' (cited by Lecomte-Tilouine 2000: 87). Most of the rebels, it seems, were rounded up after a brief skirmish; more than 300 rebels – the majority of them probably local peasants mobilised by Lakhan Thapa - were apparently killed in action, but many others surrendered. Accounts suggest that Thapa and a handful of his colleagues were captured during a secret meeting; some 60 guns and ammunition were also apparently found and seized. The rebel leaders were put in bamboo cages and brought to Thapathali Darbar, where a summary trial was held. They were whipped and forced to sign confessions. They were then hanged in front of the Manakamana Mai temple back in Gorkha on 27 February 1877.

It is hard to know how best to characterize this movement. It could be seen as a part of the elite opposition that Whelpton identifies - given undoubted links between events that took place at the time of the Kot Massacre, when several high-ranking Magar army officers were killed either directly or indirectly by Jang Bahadur Rana, and this revolt (although admittedly it did take place nearly 30 years after the Kot Massacre) - or as a local rebellion. If the touchstone of a peasant revolt is that it is rooted in the land question, then this was certainly not a peasant revolt. Pramode Shamshere Rana suggests that 'it was the first public revolt against the dictatorial rule of Maharaj Jang Bahadur: it was a revolt by the people' (2000: 50), thereby claiming it, retrospectively, as an early popular protest against Rana rule.

It certainly drew a degree of legitimacy from the accusation that 'the regime had strengthened the position of the rich, and failed to provide justice', and from Thapa's claim to be the reincarnation of a local saint, but it was not, I suggest, a classic peasant revolt. As Whelpton remarks, 'Magar activists have portrayed Lakhan Thapa as a proto-democratic fighter against the Rana tyranny and, in 2000, the Nepalese government officially declared him a 'martyr'. The religious dimension of his revolt, however, suggests that he had more in common with earlier traditions of resistance to central authority than with twentieth-century political activism' (Whelpton 2013: 69, footnote 20).

I am not myself convinced that the so-called 'religious dimension' was much more than a device to give the opposition more legitimacy among the local population. There are numerous instances around the world of rebellions led by men who claimed to have divine support for their action, or in some cases claimed themselves to be religious figures, prophets or saints[19]. The movement can be more appropriately characterised, I suggest, as a rural rebellion, led by local notables[20].

---

19. See, for example, Bu Hmara, the 'man on a donkey' who led a rebellion against the Sultan in pre-colonial 19th century Morocco and claimed to be the legitimate Sultan and to have supernatural powers (Seddon 1978).
20. More like Kett's rebellion: a revolt in Norfolk, England during the reign of Edward VI, largely in response to the enclosure of land. It began at Wymondham on 8 July 1549 with a group of rebels destroying fences that had been put up by wealthy landowners. One of their targets was yeoman farmer Robert Kett who, instead of resisting the rebels, agreed to their demands and offered to lead them. Kett and his forces, joined by recruits from Norwich and the surrounding countryside and numbering some 16,000, set up camp on Mousehold Heath to the north-east of the city on 12 July. The rebels stormed Norwich on 29 July and took the city. But on 1 August the rebels were defeated by an army led by the Marquess of Northampton, who had been sent by the government to suppress the uprising. Kett's rebellion ended on 27 August. Kett was captured, held in the Tower of London, tried for treason, and hanged from the walls of Norwich Castle on 7 December 1549.

6

Late Rana Rule

Elite Politics

Jang Bahadur Rana himself died the same year (1877) as Lakhan Thapa's rebellion was brought to an end, bringing to a conclusion a distinctive period in Nepal's history. There followed nearly a decade of elite politics, involving plot and counterplot to determine the succession, pitting brothers against each other and cousins against cousins. Finally, in 1885, the closest male relatives of Jang Bahadur Rana - his brother Ranoddip, his son Jagat Jang and his grandson (Jagat Jang's son), Yuddha Pratap - were assassinated by the Shumsheres, the sons of Jang Bahadur's brother Dhir Shumshere, who then ruled Nepal for the next 65 years. Jang Bahadur's remaining close relatives first took refuge in the British Residency, and then managed to secure safe passage to India. Later they attempted to launch an armed attack against the new rulers; but this was unsuccessful and several of them were then put under supervision by the British Indian authorities. This was perhaps the clearest example of 'elite politics' since the Kot massacre nearly half a century before.

Rural Unrest in the Eastern Hills

In the latter part of the 19th century, Whelpton notes, as evidence of ethnic unrest, that 'the Limbus, a much more homogeneous group than the Rais to their west, succeeded better than other

Tibeto-Burman groups in retaining their traditional *kipat* system of communal landholding, at least up until 1886'. In that year, however, legislation was passed which provided for the conversion of all land granted by Limbus to non-Limbus. There was, as a result of this government intervention, 'rising Limbu discontent' over the amount of land now being permanently lost to 'their community' – and in some parts of Limbuwan such was the level of dissension and dissent that it proved impossible to complete revenue surveys after 1893. The effective refusal of the government's proposed legislation was a form of rural protest, resistance verging on rebellion.

Caplan states that there followed several attempts to organize opposition among the Limbus to stem the tide of *kipat* conversion to *raikar* tenure by the government (Caplan 2000: 175, cited in Karki 2002: 9). The result of this dissidence, interestingly, was a major concession: new legislation in 1901 forbade the permanent alienation of any *kipat* land to a non-Limbu. But this must have proved ineffective, for in 1913 and in 1917, the *subbas* of Ilam forged an alliance to combat continuing land alienation. According to Caplan, over 300 men - mainly *subbas* – came forward and challenged the government's policies with regard to *kipat* tenure, leading to the withdrawal of proposals to abolish it altogether. The *subbas* were able to maintain this alliance, and in fact formed an ad hoc committee to defend their traditional *kipat* tenure, throughout the first half of the 20th century. This is clearly another example (like that of the *birta* owners in the *terai* referred to previously) of local elites challenging the authority of the state, on behalf of their peasant communities, and of rural folk more generally defying the state.

Whelpton insists on framing this intriguing example of resistance to government land and taxation policy solely in 'ethnic' terms, which is of course how the leaders of the unrest characterised it; but it can also be seen as a rebellion, a form of resistance to state authority and as a peasant movement, in so far as it mobilized cultivators around the issue of land and land rights. This movement, however one wishes to characterize it, was clearly associated with strong resistance by local leaders and peasant farmers, with their own distinctive form of *kipat* communal tenure, to government intervention to legitimize the alienation of their communal heritage.

The ability to maintain effective organized local resistance to intervention of this kind by the Rana regime was clearly linked to the communal basis of land tenure in the far eastern hills, the relatively egalitarian nature of local economy and society, and the tradition of local chiefs and resistance from the time of 'unification' onwards to further integration into the state. In other words, their ability to resist further encroachment was linked to a combination of political ideology (ethnicity and egalitarianism) and political economy (community-based economy and society). It was also, on the other side, linked to the difficulties of deploying state force to ensure compliance in such a difficult and relatively remote region against determined local resistance. In other parts of the Rana state, the 'reach' of the state was greater and more effective.

'The Cultivation of Maize'

On the other hand, there were increasing signs of discontent, not only among the rural population but among the Nepali intelligentsia. One person who bridged that 'divide' was Subba Krishna Lal Adhikari, a landowner and farmer from Kathmandu, who wrote a small pamphlet innocuously entitled 'Makaiko Kheti' (*The Cultivation of Maize*), which created a real stir. Although the book was ostensibly about how to cultivate corn technically and scientifically, it also made use of various metaphors to allude to the oppressive regime of the Ranas and Brtish imperialism. For example, he referred to 'domestic and foreign dogs', and to 'the devils that had entered since 1846'. More specifically he wrote about 'the red headed insects and the black headed insects' that ate the farmers' maize. This particularly offended Chandra and Bhim Shamsher Rana, because they wore red and black topis respectively. Adhikari also commented that 'Chandro daya[21] is not as good as mother's milk to a child'. Two pundits at the court of Chandra Shumshere — Ramhari Adhikari and Bhojraj Kafle – accused him of treason.

Adhikari was sentenced to a nine-year prison sentence by a court decision of 2 August 1920. He was informed, however, that his term of imprisonment could be lessened to six years if he returned all 1,000 copies of the book. He is said to have returned all but the one copy. Adhikari died in jail after three years. There is no record of Adhikari's defence, although it is claimed that he had in fact sought permission to publish; nor is his response to the accusation of treason [*bagyan*] levelled against him. The whole episode remains somewhat of a mystery. The book is still remembered in Nepal as the first book heralding demand for change. The episode, however, effectively discouraged critical writing about the Ranas for some years, and it was not until a decade later that the first political organization formed with the express aim of overthrowing the Ranas – the Prachanda Gorkha - was established.

Yogmaya

The eastern hills, however, were to see yet another instance of rural protest when, in the early 1920s and 1930s, a Brahmin widow from Bhojpur led a movement opposing caste discrimination and oppression, and against the many other forms of state injustice, which lasted from the third decade of the century until the 1940s.

21. Daya is a Nepali girl's name meaning kindness or mercy.

This is one of the few rural protest movements led by a woman and with large numbers of active female participants, although women have always been important, if often invisible, participants in rural protest[22].

Yogmaya Neupane was born as Maya Devi into a Brahmin family in Simle village in Nepaledada VDC between 1860 and 1868, the only daughter (and sister to two young boys). She was married very young to a Koirala boy. She was widowed within three years of her wedding, badly treated (as a *poi-tokuwi*) by her in-laws, and eventually returned home. She developed a secret liaison with a local Brahmin boy and eventually eloped, leaving home (and Nepal) to marry him in Assam. When he died some ten years later, she married again. Widowed for a third time, Yogmaya, who by now had a daughter, Nainakala, decided to adopt a life of renunciation and live the rest of her life as an ascetic. While it was fairly common for males to become ascetics in Hindu society at the time, it was very rare for females to do so.

She returned to Nepal around 1916 with her daughter to her home village and handed over daughter Nainakala to her brother and his wife. In this way she gave up all her responsibilities and assumed the life of an ascetic in Majuwa Besi in Bhojpur where she set up an *ashram* and is said to have meditated naked or wrapped in a single piece of cloth in a cave. It was during this period that Yogmaya began composing her religious songs and poems[23]. Analysis of her early works suggests that she was heavily

22. This account relies in part on accounts published by Barbara Aziz (1993, 2001) and in part on a summary by Michael Hutt in a lecture (2015).
23. Yogmaya and her daughter Nainakala were illiterate. Her poems were compiled and published by her literate disciples. In fact, the *Yogbani* is considered to be only a small part of her collection of poems, which she continued to compose until the year of her *jal samadhi* (1941). The collection is known as *Sarvartha Yogbani*.

influenced by the principles of reformist Hindu leader Dayananda Saraswati, who was very popular in India at the time Yogmaya was living in Assam.

She began to attract followers or disciples, who called her Shakit Hajoor and Shakti Maya. Many of her followers were from the *dalit* community. During 1917 to 1918, she travelled as an ascetic within Nepal and came in contact with many renowned religious leaders, including Swargadwari Mahaprabhu Abhayananda Second, who admired her devotion and guided her in her Yogic spiritual education. She then returned to her home village to practice her *sadhana*.

Her previous personal experiences, and the discrimination she had faced as a widow, deeply affected her outlook on what she saw as the injustices of Hindu society in Nepal. Despite being a follower and preacher of Hindu spirituality, she made it clear in her songs and poems that the patriarchal caste-based society was unacceptably harsh towards women, lower caste groups and the poor and disadvantaged more generally. Her literary works, which were directed at the women, peasants and workers of Bhojpur, are well reflected in the poem, '*Maharaj Chhan Darbarma Herna Aaundainan; Dukhi Janle Niya Nishaf Sidha Paudainan*', which criticizes the regime for its lack of compassion for the suffering of the poor and lack of justice. Her particular focus was the exploitation and oppression of women. This resonated with an increasing number of people – mainly women.

She formed and became the first chair-person of the Nepal *nari samiti* in 1918. Her local following grew through the 1920s, and after the publication of her poems, people from as far away as Darjeeling and Kathmandu began to join become her disciples; she now had thousands of followers. The local elite – including landowners and state officials - began to find her a significant threat and attempted to contain her influence. Yogmaya, whose utterances are carefully yet incompletely preserved in *Sarvartha Yogbani* published from Assam after her death, explicitly condemned caste discrimination and corrupt Brahmins, moneylenders, jagirdars, and the rulers. She sent petitions to Bir Shumsher, Chandra Shumsher and Juddha Shumsher demanding alms and *dharma-rajya*. She warned the rulers that apocalypse was near for them.

In 1931, Yogmaya sent one of her disciples, Prem Narayan Bhandari, to Kathmandu to spread the word. Learning of this, the then Prime Minister of Nepal, Juddha Shumshere Rana, met with Bhandari and promised he would take Yogmaya's message seriously. There was little change, however, over the next four years and so, in 1936, Yogmaya once again sent Bhandari to Kathmandu; and this time she herself also travelled to Kathmandu, with her daughter.

During her visit she had an audience with Juddha Shumshere, at which he reportedly asked what she wanted, and she replied: 'the alms of the holy order of truth and justice'. Then, before leaving the Kathmandu Valley, Yogmaya handed him a 24-point appeal detailing the reforms she and her followers wanted to see in the country. This alarmed Juddha Shumshere and his circle, who, already concerned by growing political dissent, began to see Yogmaya and her movement as an additional threat.

Rising Resistance to Rana Rule

Already, the regime had grounds for concern: increasing discontent among the Nepali intelligentsia at home and abroad from the 1920s onwards, the establishment in 1932 of the Prachanda Gorkha – a group of young Nepalis who planned to bomb all senior Ranas, but were arrested before they could implement their plans, and then exiled or jailed - and the formation in 1935 of the Praja Parishad – a party that espoused democracy and a constitutional monarchy. Back in Bhojpur, Yogmaya and her movement were now constantly monitored.

Prachanda Gorkha was formed with the objective of overthrowing the Ranas. The plan, apparently, was to wipe out the Ranas by bombing them while they were traveling through Dilli Bazar, while a soldier was to eliminate Juddha Shamsher, the commander-in-chief. While searching for somebody to establish a link with the King, the activists discovered Laxman Raja, who had the same intention, although contrasting views on the precise method of execution. Due to their differences, however, Raja ended up betraying the activists, who were then arrested by the Ranas. During their trial, it became clear that the activists had been inspired by revolutionary ideas. This led to some of them being sentenced to life imprisonment, others to house arrest and 'home detention', and in some cases, banishment from the Valley.

Although they had failed to achieve their objectives, the Prachanda Gorkha reflected and expressed the deep injustices prevalent in Nepal under the Ranas. In the meanwhile, for her part, Yogmaya was becoming increasingly vocal in opposition to the regime, declaring that now it was time to begin a new era by destroying the injustices, superstitions and corrupt practices that so adversely affected Nepali society. She added that she herself was nearing her own 'salvation' and would demonstrate this – and bring even more moral pressure to bear on the regime - by preparing for a human sacrifice in which she and hundreds of her disciples would be burned to death in a ritual called *agni samadhi* on Kartik Shukla Purnima (12 November 1938).

Fearing widespread rural unrest if such a mass sacrifice were allowed to happen, Juddha Shumsere ordered the disruption of the event by deploying around 500 security personnel at the selected place on 11 November, following which eleven male disciples were jailed at Dhankuta and most of the female would-be participants in the *agni samadhi* ritual, including Yogmaya and Nainakala, were confined to the Radhakrishna Temple at Bhojpur. The women were released after three months, and most of the men three years later, in April 1941.

After the release of all her disciples, Yogmaya decided to continue with her self-sacrificing plans, but this time the plans were to remain a secret. She set a new date for a *jal samadhi* – 5 July 1941, which was the day of the holy Harisayani Ekadasi - and allowed only a select group of disciples to join her. The religious ritual for the *jal samadhi* began on the night of 4 July 1941 and in the morning of 5 July at around 4 am, Yogmaya led the ritualistic mass suicide by climbing on a rock placing a plate with lighted oil lamps on her head on the bank of the Arun River. After Yogmaya, some 65 of her disciples jumped on the river in succession that morning, and the next day two more followed suit. Ultimately, the total death count from the event stood at 68[24].

---

24. Information about Yogmaya and the mass suicide was strictly censored by the Rana regime. Even after its overthrow, during the Panchayat era, it remained difficult to discuss her legacy. Yet, her disciples, mainly in the districts of Bhojpur, Khotang and Sankhuwasabha, maintained the tradition locally. Some of Yogmaya's female disciples continued to live in the Manakamana Temple in Tumlingtar. More recently, however, scholars, including Barbara Nimri Aziz, Michael Hutt and Dipesh Neupane, have carried out research and published their findings on Yogmaya and her rural movement.

    Topics on Yogmaya and her movement have been also included in the curricula of sociology, anthropology and women's studies at several universities in Nepal.A local organization has been formed in Bhojpur, called the 'Yogamaya Shakti Pith Tapobhumi Bikash Tatha Vikas Sanstha', to promote her work and activities as well as preserve the places where Yogmaya spent a significant time during her ascetic life - around Nepaledada and Dingla. On 8 March 2011, to mark International Women's Day, a statue of Yogmaya Neupane was unveiled in the district headquarters town of Bhojpur. This was the latest development in an

Political Opposition

In October 1940, another political organization – the Praja Parishad – was formed; but its leaders were quickly arrested and charged with plotting the assassination of the Rana family. Four were sentenced to death and others to long jail sentences. This was, however, essentially a movement of disaffected sections of the emerging 'urban middle classes' and not based in rural discontent. It was not until the foment of the Quit India movement in India to the south and the rise of Indian nationalism spurred on the establishment of both the Nepali Congress and the Communist Party in India in the 1940s that a systematic opposition – in the rural as well as the urban areas - to continued Rana rule was created.

The communist movement of Nepal really began to take shape after the publication of the Nepali edition of the Communist Manifesto in April 1949 – the year that the Communist Party of China came to power and Mao Tse Tung began to re-formulate Marxist-Leninist thought to identify the peasantry, and especially the 'middle peasantry', as a revolutionary class. Interestingly, the very first two lines of the Communist Party manifesto were: '*pahad parbat khola nala jamin sabkho; malik hami dash banau hisha shabko* (the mountains, rivers, streams and land are ours; we are the masters – why should we be slaves – we all have a share in our heritage (CPN 1949, cited in Karki 2002: 9). This was a somewhat rural version of 'workers of the world unite! You have nothing to lose but your chains'.

The first leaflet produced by the CPN in April 1949 declared that Nepal should establish a 'new democracy', as in China – if

---

iconisation process that constructs and promotes Yogmaya as Nepal's first female revolutionary. On November 16, 2016, the Government issued a postal stamp in recognition of her contributions to the history of Nepal.

necessary through armed struggle – so as to create a People's Republic'. It explained that 'the peasants have to struggle to assuage their hunger, increase the value of their farm produce and their wages, and own their own land. So, they want liberation'. It is reminiscent of the call of the original Communist Manifesto which promised workers of the world that if they were to unite they had only their chains to lose. The manifesto of the CPN stated that 'your freedom is possible only by means of a powerful and uncompromising struggle against the existing feudal system'; it also argued that 'there is a need to create a people's organization throughout the country, under the leadership of the red flag, and to launch a struggle to achieve the demand - 'land to the tillers' – made by the CPN' (see Dhakal 2018: 13).

The Communist Party of Nepal (CPN) was formally established in Calcutta in September 1949. The objective of the CPN was 'to oppose the autocratic Rana regime, feudalism and imperialism'. Its manifesto called for 'the total abolition of the feudal autocratic regime' which meant 'the elimination of all kinds of feudal exploitation, including the landlord system, and the distribution of land among the tillers of the land, repayment of rural loans, and wages for agricultural labourers sufficient to ensure them a decent living' (Pushpa Lal vs 2055; Rawal 2007).

The next year, in April 1950, a merger of the Nepali National Congress (founded in 1947) under B. P. Koirala and the Nepali Democratic Congress (formed in 1949), led to the establishment of the Nepali Congress Party. Even before this, in 1946, the Kishan Sangh (Peasants Association) was secretly formed in Rautahat and in 1947, according to Sadhana Adhikari (wife of Man Mohan Adhikari, quoted in Pandey & Rimal n.d.: 14), the Nepal Women's Association was founded, and over the next two years demanded votes for women (a demand which bore fruit in 1952) and education for women. Apparently, large numbers of peasant women joined the Association, and in 1949 a peasants' conference was held in the house of her *nati dai* with more than 20 peasant women actively participating. Peasant women continued to be actively involved in the Nepal Women's Association throughout the next decade[25].

The Overthrow of the Ranas

In 1950, King Mahendra sought refuge in the Indian Embassy, and then fled to India. The rebel forces of the Nepali Congress crossed the border into Nepal and launched an attack on the district headquarters at Birgunj, where the garrison soon surrendered. Leaflets, and the party manifesto, written by B. P. Koirala in 1950, were dropped from the air over Kathmandu at the beginning of the revolt. These promised loyalty to a constitutional monarchy, the introduction of democracy 'as in the west' and social reforms. Throughout the next month, the armed insurrection of the Jana Mukti Sena (People's Liberation Army) developed and spread, picking up support from within the country, in part from the defection of Rana troops to the rebels.

The defection of the Palpa garrison in western Nepal in early January 1951 was a notable 'coup' for the rebels; but they also proved able to overcome or drive out the small and generally ill-trained army garrisons from the hill towns where they tended to be located. The rebels were supported by a local uprising against the Rana regime in the eastern hills. Civil unrest in Kathmandu, Pokhara and several towns in the *terai* also supported and complemented the armed struggle against the regime. In the meanwhile, the king and the Indian government came to terms on their own, ensuring that the overthrow of the old regime would not be as complete as the opposition had intended.

25. The Nepal Women's Association was not the same as the All Nepal Women's Association set up by Punya Prabha Dunghana in 1951

What came to be known as 'the Delhi Compromise' led to an agreement (between the Rana government, the King and the Indian government) whereby the king would play the role of a constitutional monarch, under a new democratic Constitution (to be framed by a Constituent Assembly elected by the people). The last part of this agreement was never honoured: an interim government was formed in February 1951 to carry out the task, but the king refused to allow the framing of a new democratic constitution[26].

---

26. His successor, King Mahendra, who came to the throne in 1955, also failed to honour the Royal Proclamation.

7

Rural Unrest in the 1950s

Generalized dissidence

Karki (2002) observes that 'immediately after the political changes of the 1950s, Nepali peasants in some parts of the country were involved in the armed struggle conducted by the Nepali Congress and the Communist Party. This was the first time farmers began to confiscate the land of feudal landlords with the slogan 'Land to the Tillers'.

In fact, the early 1950s constituted a period of generalized dissidence characterized not only by the efforts of political activists from outside Nepal at the very beginning of the decade to remove the Ranas from power, but also by a plethora of smaller and less orchestrated peasant movements. Some of these were linked to these new 'revolutionary' political parties and to the newly formed Peasant Associations, like the Krishi Sudhar Sangh (Agriculture Reform Association, AFA or Association for Agricultural Improvement, AAI) and the Kishan-Majdor Sangh (Peasant-Worker Association (PWA) – which united to form the Akhil Nepal Kishan Sangh (All Nepal Peasant Association, ANPA) in 1952, by which time it had spread to 24 of the 35 districts of Nepal (Karki 2002: 9).

A couple of peasant associations were active during the Rana regime (ie prior to 1951, like the Krishi Sudhar Sangh (Association for Agricultural Improvement) and the Kishan-Majdooor Sangh (Peasants and Workers Association) (INSEC 1995; Tuladhar 2000, cited in Suresh Dhakal (2013: 132). Political parties were also involved in promoting agrarian change in favour of peasants and agricultural labourers. The Nepali Congress Party, for example, argued that the unequal distribution of land ownership was unjustified and unjustifiable and in favour of a re-distribution of the land: 'in Nepali Congress' view, the land held by big landlords and *birta* holders should be distributed to hardworking peasants and farm labourers' (Dhakal 2018: 14). Even the Nepal Rastrabadi Gorkha Parishad (formerly the Gorkha Dal), founded in 1951 as a pro-monarchy party representing the landowning class, was committed to lowering rents and interest rates and waiving debts (Dhakal 2018: 15).

B.P. Koirala urged that 'the Nepali Congress should clearly spell out that our organization does good to the peasants' and argued that 'we have to replace the old feudal land tenure system by such a system under which the peasants working on the farm will have rights to the land' (Tuladhar 2046 vs). Despite this, Koirala arguably 'not only dismissed peasants' issues but also suppressed their voices' during the three terms of his premiership between 1951 and 1954; indeed, Tuladhar argues that peasant revolts and uprisings were 'brutally suppressed' during the 1950s as the landlords had not only a strong influence but arguably a decisive role in forming and dissolving the government in those years. Furthermore, landlords organized in other ways to combat rural unrest and suppress peasant movements – which included Birtwal Sangh (in 2008 vs), Bhumijibi Sangh (2010 vs) and Janahit Sangh (2016 vs) according to Dhakal (2018: 16).

Karki also remarks that 'the government used nomadic tribals and the Indian Army to suppress these movements, who were pressing the government to form a Land Examination Comission in 1952 and a Land Reform Commission in 1953 (Shrestha 1977: 28). But the first Congress of the Communist Party (26-30 January 1954) passed a resolution demanding the confiscation of land and farm implements from feudal landlords and their distribution to peasants and landless people' (CPN 1954, cited in Karki 2002: 9).

Unrest in Bhaktapur, Kathmandu Valley

In Bhaktapur, peasant unrest broke out in Somlingtar in 1950-51 with a focus on the rights of tenants and the non-payment of grain (*kutbali*)[27]. There were other, related instances of unrest in Kathmandu and Bhaktapur later the same year. Jagat Basnet suggests that 'the movement of Bhaktapur proceeded in an organized way and focused on *birta, jamindari* system and the rights of tenants' (Basnet 2008: 21) The demands of the peasants included the abolition of landlordship and the *talukdari* system. These actions by local peasants led to the formation by the Communist Party of a peasant or farmers' association – the Akhil Nepal Kishan Sangh (the All Nepal Peasants' Association - ANPA) – whose main concern was to combat the control exerted over the peasantry by *birta* owners and *zamindars,* and which advocated the 'rights of the tillers'.

According to Basnet et al (2010: 119), the refusal of tenants in Somlingtar in Bhaktapur to pay rents in the form of grain payments 'set off a movement against share-cropping in Rajapur, Bardiya District; the *jamindar birodhi andolan* in Lumbini; the *dharma bhakari andolan* in Bara and Rautahat Districts; led to an organized and focused movement against the *birta* tenure system and the *jamindari* system, and in support of tenancy rights; (and) inspired the formation of an agricultural union parallel to the

27. Under the *kut* system, the cultivator paid a stipulated quantity of food grain or other commodities, or a stipulated sum in cash.

Akhil Nepal Kishan Sangh'. Basnet states that 'in 1951, Basu Pasa, a farmer leader from Bhaktapur, formed a separate organization called Krishni Sudhar Sangh, claiming that the common farmers' association (ie the Akhil Nepal Kishan Sangh) was controlled only by the communists (Thapa 2001)' (Basnet 2008: 21)[28]. Basupasa had been middle-zone committee chair of the All Nepal Peasants Association (ANPA), but he resigned as soon as it was formed, because he believed that the communists had captured the organization, even though it had been established jointly by the Nepali Congress Party, the Communist Party of Nepal and the Praja Parishad.

Basu Pasa argued that 'two parallel governments could not go simultaneously. There was also the issue of the dual arrangement for collecting land tax. Land tax should be collected only by the government of Nepal and not by the master of the *birta* owners' (Basnet 2008: 22). According to Basnet, demonstrations by peasants in Kathmandu and Bhaktapur against the government in October 1954 produced six demands, including the abolition of the landlord system. Some 19 protestors were arrested at these demonstrations. Karki (2002: 10) states that 'this helped to mobilise peasants of Kathmandu Valley who engaged in the struggle, demanding that the *guthi* should accept payment of half cash and half kind instead of claiming two thirds in rice and one third in cash. They further demanded that the date of paying the crop contribution be extended up to the middle of March. The action policy and objective of these struggles was explained in a 12-point programme, including the distribution of public land to local landless people'.

28. Budhathoki states that the Akhil Nepal Kishan Sangh Suddikaran Samiti (All Nepal Peasants Association Reform Committee, ANPARC) was formed as a breakaway from the ANPA on 8 February 1955, with Padam Bahadur Budathoki as chairman and Basupasa as general secretary (Buddhathoki 2048 vs; 1981: 8).).

This paved the way for a second phase of the revolt in March 1957, following which 55 peasants were arrested and detained (Basnet et al 2010: 119). These peasant movements in Bhaktapur continued, according to Thapa (2001), in one form or another, until the 1980s; and, certainly, the formation in 1975 of the Workers and Peasants Party under the leadership of Narayan Man ('Comrade Rohit') Bijukche both reflected and contributed to the continuing importance of the peasant movement in Bhaktapur up to the present day. The strong association of Bhaktapur with peasant unrest and protest is linked to the dominance of locals who identify themselves as Jyapu, which can be translated as 'farmer' or 'peasant' or seen as a term referring rather to a caste or ethnic group – indeed, David Gellner has argued that in the case of Bhaktapur and the Workers and Peasants Party, 'communism can be an ideology which masks a kind of Jyapu ethnicity' (1997, cited in Thapa, S. 2013: 168).

Bhaktapur remains a 'special case', and a history of the specifics of the peasant movement there, and of the Workers and Peasants Party, is long over-due.

Unrest in the Eastern Hills

The armed insurrection or rebellion against the Ranas in the eastern hills at the beginning of the decade was largely organized by Rai and Limbu ex-servicemen, many of whom were also reasonably comfortable 'middle peasants', and was centred in Bhojpur, where rebels under Naradmuni Thulung (Rai) seized control on 9 December 1950, setting up a provisional government and dispatching forces to seize other towns in the eastern hills. A government force sent to re-capture Bhojpur was defeated and the commander summarily executed. The rebels extended their control eastwards into Sakhuwasabha, Dankhuta, Terathum and Taplejung; south through into the eastern *terai;* and westwards to Dhulikel on the edge of the Kathmandu Valley (Whelpton provides a map on p. 41).

Although there was undoubtedly communication between the Nepali Congress and Naradmuni Thulung's revolt, and Naradmuni himself had been recruited earlier into Koirala's Nepali National Congress, he and his followers effectively acted on their own initiative and this can, I believe, be seen as a local rebellion or revolt, exemplifying into the 20th century a continuation of the strong tradition in the eastern hills of resistance to state authority emanating from Kathmandu that had been visible from the very early days of 'unification' in the late 18th century. This rebellion, however, was led by someone with important links with 'the centre' and not just by some peasant or ex-serviceman.

Naradmuni was a well-known and respected figure in Bhojpur as he had established the first English school there in 1947, making good use, ironically, of his connections with the Ranas to secure funds from the government, and had also been nominated as one of two eastern Nepal representatives on a committee supervising the use of a fund for war orphans set up with money from the British government. When Congress was about to launch its invasion from India, Mohan Shumshere Rana wrote to Naradmuni and his uncle Harka Raj, asking for their help in defending the regime, and even after Naradmuni and his supporters had effectively staged a bloodless coup in Bhojpur, the Bada Hakim, not realizing this, handed his own gun over to Naradmuni and told him to fight the rebels!

As the campaign developed, the rebels were able – as the Maoists would do decades later – to capture weapons from government forces and also to rely on substantial local popular support. Whelpton remarks that 'there is evidence, however, of a degree of coercion, as with the later Maoist insurgency:

'proceedings' (*karyabahi*) were threatened against those unwilling to provide provisions for the Mukti Sena and, although it was finally decided not to make unarmed civilians accompany the assault force, in the run-up to the second assault on Okhaldhunga in mid-January 1951, the local population was threatened with death if they did not assemble at a nearby crossing on the Dudh Khosi (Karki 2008: 102, cited in Whelpton 2013: 42).

Talks between the rebels and the Rana government were held in mid-January 1951 in Delhi and a ceasefire was agreed by the Indian government, King Tribhuvan and the Mohan Shumshere Rana regime. By the time fighting stopped in February 1951, Naradmuni Thulung and his fighters had secured a territory that extended from Taplejung on the Sikkim border west as far as Dhulikhel on the eastern rim of the Kathmandu Valley. This was noted with concern in Kathmandu where, apparently, people were worried that 'the Kiratas are coming!' (Karki 2008: 189). As in all cases of rural unrest in the eastern hills, 'the ethnic dimension' was important, the local peasantry was heavily involved, both voluntarily and involuntarily, but the question as to how far this can be regarded as a 'peasant movement' is debatable. It would perhaps be best to regard it as a rebellion, and a local contribution to the struggle against the Rana regime.

It was, however, a typically local insurgency, with a tendency for individual units to go off in their own direction, even if they were under the overall direction of the high command under Naradmuni. The initial capture of Okhaldunga, for example, was achieved by Mughadan Rai, who gathered armed supporters and effectively acted on his own after failing to maintain adequate contact with the principal leaders of the movement. There were several cases of friction between different groups of insurgents trying to operate against the same target and even an internal revolt within the movement itself, led by Dhan Bahadur Rai, who won over some of the fighters still in Bhojpur to his side, and put both Naradmuni and his main collaborator, Ram Prasad Rai, under arrest on 6 March 1951.

Naradmuni's authority was only fully restored when B. P. Koirala, then Home Minister in the new coalition government, ordered the intervention of J.B. Yakthumba, a leader of the Mukti Sena that had been originally organised in India to provide support. The interim Bhojpur government, like the administration set up by Narendranath Bastola and his colleagues in Ilam, continued to function more or less independently of the government in Kathmandu until B. P. Koirala himself negotiated their dissolution during visits to the eastern region in the summer of 1951.

Krishna Prasad Bhattarai, who took part in the armed movement himself, once told an interviewer that the difficulty of keeping their fighters under control was the principal reason why the Nepali Congress accepted a ceasefire in January 1951. Whelpton suggests that 'the crucial factor was probably the pressure on Congress from India to accept the compromise that India had itself proposed, and which King Tribhuvan and the Ranas had already agreed to'; but he also accepts that 'Bhattarai's words underscore the fact that discipline was a problem both within the eastern hills insurrection and elsewhere' (Whelpton 2013: 43).

This tendency for local groups to act more or less independently and even to shift allegiance to other emerging dissident groups was a feature of several other movements that developed in the year or so after the overthrow of the Ranas, while the awkward new political dispensation was in play. For example, Mukti Sena members from Bhojpur who were recruited into the Raksha Dal, an auxiliary security force set up immediately after the overthrow of the Ranas, were also at the heart of the brief Raksha Dal revolt led by K. I. Singh in January 1952.

Unrest in the Far West

The armed struggle against the Ranas led to the establishment of a 'revolutionary government' in several areas, including the far west. Thapa states that 'in November 1950, the revolutionary government of western Nepal declared the end of the *bataiya* (sharecropping) and *hunda* systems, and distributed all such lands to the cultivators'. He remarks that this must be seen as a truly revolutionary development, but comments that 'unfortunately, the democratic government formed after the tri-partite agreement signed in New Delhi ordered to return all such lands to the landlords' (Thapa 1996: 75; Thapa 2001: 119, cited in Basnet & Upreti 2008: 245).

This 'revolutionary government' was that of Bhim Dutta Panta. Panta had been involved in the Indian freedom movement – having links with Indian peasant uprisings such as Tebhaga, Nijaibole and Telangana - and, according to Pokharel and Basyal (1999: 155) was detained in India for 18 months because of this. Karki suggests that Panta was 'the first person who tried to organize these landless people into a movement against semi-feudal production relations in western Nepal. Locals think that he was a communist leader with strong ties to Indian revolutionaries. Since he was one of the activists involved in the Indian freedom movement, he had established good contacts with people related to peasant uprisings such as tebhaga, Nijaibole and Telangana. However, his contact with Kathmandu and leaders of other social and political movements in Nepal seems limited' (Karki 2002: 10)

Panta had joined the Nepali Congress Party in October 1949 and then organized and mobilized the local peasants and agricultural workers and became a target for the local landowners and for the Rana government. He was very unpopular with local landlords, who tried unsuccessfully to kill him. He was caught by them on several occasions, but freed because of public pressure. He was then involved in the movement against the Ranas in 1950, operating firstly in Dadeldhura and Baitadi, Bajhang and Bhadura in the far western hills and then in Kailali and Kanchanpur in the far western *terai.*

In February 1951, he was made governor of the Mahakali region by the new coalition government. He continued, however, to be a committed radical, opposed to all forms of bonded labour, including *haliya* and *kamaiya*, and supported the idea of 'the rights of the tillers' (ANPA 2004). He raised awareness among the local peasant and workers with the slogan: 'either you cultivate the land or you leave' (INSEC 1995, cited in Basnet 2008: 23). The slogan frightened the feudal landlords, but more and more farmers became involved in the movement. He apparently continued to lead a simple life, even though governor, often taking salt, rice and clothing from the black market and distributing them to the poor. He recruited all kinds of people, including Tharus and Magars from Kailali and Kanchanpur, to his cause. One of his popular slogans was: *kita jota halo; kite chhoda thalo; nafra bhaye aaba chhaina bhalo* (either you plough the land or you leave the land; otherwise you will be in trouble).

He left the Nepali Congress, because he could not agree with the party's compromises, as he saw them; he joined the Communist Party after he met Krishnaswami Adkar from India (CSRC 2008, cited in Basnet 2008: 23). He dedicated himself to the peasant movement throughout the country from the beginning of 1952. Even the new government came to regard him as a 'dangerous radical communist', issuing a warrant for his arrest and a reward of

5,000 *rupees* for his life (ANPA 2004, cited in Basnet 2008: 22). The government of India was also concerned about his activities and his connections. Attempts were made to arrest him in March 1951. He was, however, recognized and supported by Nepali communist party leaders, Pushpa Lal and Man Mohan Adhikari, and he recruited some 500 young militants to join his struggle against the landowning class and for a revolution (ANPA 2004, cited in Basnet 2008: 23).

He attacked the Bada Hakim of the region, Mohan Bahadur Singh, for having sponsored the production of fake *tamasuk* (contract) documents through Gun Raj Panta (ANPA 2004), and was arrested and sent to Kanchanpur jail. But he escaped and ran away into the Jogbudha jungle. He was arrested again in February 1953 and imprisoned in Belauri jail in Kanchanpur. His peasant supporters managed have him freed in July, only for him to be arrested again a few days later. Then it was announced on the radio that he had fled by 'devastating the jail' (INSEC 1995, cited in Basnet 2008: 24); and Nepal's army chief, Kiran Shumshere Rana, announced a reward of (variously 500 rupees and 5,000 rupees, according to different accounts – Karki 2002: 10, ANPA 2004, INSEC 2005) for Bhim Dutta Panta, alive or dead.

It is said that the entire local police force, aided by troops from both the Nepal and Indian armies searched for him. But Panta apparently disguised himself by shaving off his beard, hair and eyebrows and continued to harass the landlords, aided by the locals (and his relatives) who protected him. On one occasion, it is said that secret agents discovered his whereabouts and the Indian Army encircled the place on three sides; there was a clash between the Indian Army and Bhim Dutta Panta's supporters, and many were killed on both sides; but Panta managed to escape. Spies were deployed, however, and eventually on 25 July 1953 (or according to other sources on 1 July 1954) he was found and arrested at Budar village in Doti[29] where he was seeking refuge[30].

Allegedly, he was betrayed by the locals (and his relatives) who were tempted by the reward offered for him. He was taken to the nearby jungle and severely tortured before being beheaded with a *kukhuri* by a policeman. It is said that he knew he was finished and cried out: 'I wanted to be free from feudalist oppression' and repeated this until his head was cut off. News of his death spread rapidly, and the local landowners celebrated as if for a festival. His head was hung on a bamboo with a note saying: 'your head will also hang like this if you take part in mutiny or treason'; and then brought to Khalanga and paraded around.

Some 300 of his followers were also arrested and some of these, about 50, were not released until 1956 (INSEC 1995, cited in Basnet 2008: 22). Panta's wife, his family and friends asked for his head, but Mohan Bahadur Singh abused them and forced them to sign a 31 point document committing them to keep the peace. Only then was his head released, and the funeral rites could be held at the temple of Gatal Baba in Dadeldhura. The local landlords celebrated this incident as their victory (INSEC 1995, cited in Basnet 2008: 22,2422).

Unrest in the Western Terai

Bardiya had experienced a significant transformation in landownership through the 1920s and 1930s as the area of

29. Or, alternatively, in Dadeldhura (Karki 2002: 10).
30. Adhikari comments on this incident as follows: 'in the Danghadi district of western Nepal on the Indo-Nepal border, about 700 armed men under the leadership of Bhim Dutta Pant, described as followers of K.I.Singh, let loose a reign of terror (sic). The incapacity of the government was once more exhibited when it was forced to ask for military assistance from India to suppress the rebel. During July 1953 a joint operation by the Indo-Nepal troops succeeded' (Adhikari 2015: 88).

cultivable land under control of local people was systematically reduced by land appropriation by Ranas and others, continuing a process that had started in the 1860s when Bardiya had been granted as *birta* land to Jung Bahadur Rana when the four districts of the *naya muluk* (new territory) were handed back to Nepal by the British East India Company in recognition of the support provided during the 'Great Mutiny' to suppress the uprising in northern India (Dhakal 2013: 135).

In Bardiya, the land survey of 1946-47 identified 81,000 *bighas* as cultivable land; of this, 68,000 *bighas* were owned by large landlords and only 13,000 *bighas* by smaller farmers and peasants. Adhikari comments on this incident as follows: 'in the Danghadi district of western Nepal on the Indo-Nepal border, about 700 armed men under the leadership of Bhim Dutta Pant, described as followers of K. I. Singh, let loose a reign of terror (sic). The incapacity of the government was once more exhibited when it was forced to ask for military assistance from India to suppress the rebel. During July 1953 a joint operation by the Indo-Nepal troops succeeded' (Adhikari 2015: 88).

After the survey team had returned to Kathmandu, the landlords began to seize even the relatively small amount of land owned by the peasants and, inspired by the Baiganya Declaration of the Nepali Congress Party, a local man, Radha Krishna Tharu, began in the late 1940s to organize small farmers and peasants to resist this land expropriation and to demand one third as a fair share of the product of tenant labour (*ti bhaga bataiya*). The peasant movement was suppressed brutally by the landlords, who met in Nanpada in India to form an organization to resist the efforts by the peasants to claim a fairer share of the land and of the fruits of their labours.

In 1951, after the overthrow of the Ranas, the government sent a commission to Bardiya, and also to Banke, Kailali and

Butwal districts to inquire into the many land disputes that had arisen in recent years (Regmi 1977: 138, cited in Dhakal 2013: 136). The details of these disputes is not known and it is not clear what the outcome of these commissions of enquiry was.

A land rights movement – the Beluwa Banjari Peasants Movement – began in Dang Deokhuri District in December 1959, inspired by the Nepali Congress Party's 1959 election slogan - '*Jagga kasko? Jotneko! Ghar kasko? Potneko!* ('To whom does the land belong? To the tillers. To whom does the home belong? To the tenants'). This movement was directed against landlord 'incursions' and evictions, and involved mainly Tharus. It developed further during 1960. In an effort to contain it, one of the leaders of the movement, Gumraha Chaudhury, was murdered. The death of Gumraha further aggravated the conflict (Thapa 2001, cited in Basnet 2008: 26).

Tharu women were prominent in this movement, notably Lohani/Lahani Chadhury and Somati Chaudhury; Ratna, Kalu and Lohani/Lahani were arrested and tortured, but released after a week. 'When the landlords came to loot mustard in 1959, all of us - except old people and children - went out to defend ourselves with sticks in our hands. Lohani/Lahani suffered injuries to her back. But we were not hopeless; we did not leave the ground to the landlords. Rather we chased them and their servants away. When they came again next morning, we chased them again', said Somati Chaudhury. 'They came back again in 1960. The struggle continued throughout the month of June-July. Police assisted the landlords; they haunted the area constantly to look for people. One day, Ratna and Kalu were arrested. Gumraha was murdered. We had to fight hard to save the villagers from the *zamindars* and the police'. This particular struggle continued into the next year.

Unrest in the Western Hills

Communist influence was also beginning to grow in the western hills during the early 1950s. A leading activist in this regard was Mohan Bikram Singh, later to become a key figure in the Maoist movement in Nepal[31]. Singh was born in Kathmandu in 1935, but his father was a wealthy landowner with an estate in Pyuthan District in the western hills[32], and it was there that Singh grew up. He moved from Pyuthan to Kathmandu after finishing school and started reading left-wing literature; he was particularly influenced by political leaders who had started to emerge in India, notably the communist Rahul Sankrityayan; but joined the Nepali Congress, and took part in their actions against the Rana regime. His father also became a leader of the anti-Rana movement in Pyuthan during the early 1950s, but his father's motives as a rebel were anything but revolutionary, and his reputation as a renowned 'feudal' was considerable, even as far away as Thabang in Rolpa. In fact, he had notoriously increased his landholding by making local peasants sign false contracts.

M. B. Singh then joined the Rastriya Praja Parishad (National Democratic Party), shortly before moving to the Communist Party in December 1953. He and Khagu Lal Gurung organized a three-month training programme or 'progressive study group' in Ratamata near Dankhakwadi village in their home district of Pyuthan, with the objective of instilling the precepts and principles of communism in any of the local peasants and workers who signed up; the programme also included physical education. News of this spread, and soon some 150 participants

31. This section draws heavily on the work of Benoit Cailmail (2008-09, 2013).
32. M. B. Singh referred to his father as 'a feudal reformist' as he was against corruption and for democracy but against all kinds of socialist and communist ideology (Cailmail 2008-09: 17).

were involved. In February 1954, as the programme drew to an end, a delegation of residents from Narikot to the north of Dankhakwadi, came to see the two leaders, complaining of the abuse they had received from their local headman (*mukhiya*) and his allies, who had mis-appropriated local peasants' land by forcing them to sell it.

Accompanied by hundreds of militants recently converted to revolutionary principles and armed with sickles and cudgels, Singh and Gurung went to Narikot to persuade the *mukhiya* to return the land. After nearly a week of fruitless talks and even after some 600 peasants had mobilized, holding meetings and organizing demonstrations and processions, the landowners remained adamant, arguing the legality of the transfer of property and showing the documents signed by the persons concerned – a trick Singh's own father had played on peasants himself. Singh, therefore, opted for more radical methods: he kidnapped the main landowners and took them to Machchhi (Okharkot), his stronghold, where they would stand trial in a people's court. Realising the need to counter this decisive move, the remaining landowners of Narikot, accompanied by landowners from other villages, notably Khung, attacked the revolutionaries at Machchhi by night, with sticks, knives (*kukhuris*), swords and even rifles.

Singh and Gurung were prepared for this, however, and ambushed the attackers at the entrance to Machchhi. Armed themselves with sticks and stones, they also set their dogs on the attackers and forced them to retreat. The landowners were obliged to return the documents justifying their forced purchases of land and on 7 March 1954 the documents were destroyed. The immediate aim of the action taken by Singh, Gurung and others was a form of 'restorative justice', but in other actions taken in the same period, Singh advocated the transfer of 'land to the tiller' – a typical Naxalite slogan.

With this first victory of the communist party in Pyuthan, the 'revolutionaries' set out for the nearby villages of Bangemarot, Badikot and Tusara to spread the word about what was being claimed as a precedent. Singh and Gurung launched new protests and demonstrations during 1954, supporting peasants' rights and fighting corruption, as well as calling for the transfer of the district headquarters from Khalanga to Bijuwar. Singh even called on his own father – unsuccessfully - to restore the land he had taken from 'the tillers' to their rightful owners, an act that endeared him even more to his followers. After his father died, and Singh inherited the land, he returned the land that had been taken illegally from the peasants to them.

The peasant movement was remarkably effective within Pyuthan and particularly within the areas of Okharkot, Narikot, Bangemarot and Tusara, but appears not to have spread much beyond – although its influence may have been greater than it appeared. As regards the leadership itself, Benoit Cailmail quotes Bianco on the Chinese experience: 'the leaders [of the peasant revolts] are more frequently non-peasants than peasants, and among the latter, mostly well or fairly well-off farmers, than poor peasants' (2005: 149), and suggests that this is also the case in Nepal, at least in Pyuthan in the 1950s. He concludes that the leaders of the peasant movements in Pyuthan tended to share relatively comfortable backgrounds – although he recognizes that was a peasant, farming just over 1 hectare of land throughout his political career (Cailmail 2013: 144-147) – and had all attended school at a time when that was still exceptional.

He accepts that such generalization is difficult, and in any case, this was not the case for most of the grass-roots activists who made up the cadres and committed supporters of the movements. We shall see that similar movements, albeit on a more localized scale, were encouraged in the 1970s by young outsiders with political commitments and attachments who established a library and training for local cadres, and led a peasant movement against local landowners and government functionaries – the Chintang Bidorha (1971-1979). They too were to experience a heavy response from local elites, leading to the arrest and detention of the identified leaders (see below).

Eventually, in January 1955, while leading demonstrations in Bagdula, Singh and Gurung were surrounded by police and arrested; they were sentenced to two years in jail. Even from jail, Singh and Gurung continued to agitate for people's rights and revolutionary change. They were transferred from prison to prison, the last transfer being after they launched a rebellion inside the prison in Palpa where they were incarcerated to object to prison conditions. The wardens tried to suppress the rebellion by beating up Singh, but he fought back, striking the guards with his shoes. When the other inmates rallied round him, it was decided that, to avoid a prison riot, he and Gurung should be transferred to Salyan. When news of this event reached Pyuthan there were large demonstrations demanding his release.

He was released in 1956, and the next year was elected to the Central Committee of the CPN. Two years later, in the first democratic elections held in Nepal in 1959, the CPN secured exceptionally strong support in the area where Singh had earlier mobilised the peasantry. Indeed, the legacy of Mohan Bikram Singh and Khagu Lal Gurung in Pyuthan in particular was immense, as Benoit Cailmail notes, and remained strong throughout the Panchayat Era, through the early 1990s, when the local party was re-defined as the CPN (Masal), and during the Maoist insurgency (2013: 144-161).

Unrest in the West Central Terai

In Lumbini, a peasant movement directed against the landlords and called simply *jamindar birodhi andolan* that developed in the early 1950s, was closely linked to the activities in the area of the Nepali Congress. Before November 1950, K. I. Singh, the son of a minor Thakuri landowner, who had been educated in India and had served for some time in the Indian army, where he had acquired some medical training, set himself up as a doctor based at Nautanwa, just south of the Nepal-Indian border, He travelled extensively in Nepal's western *terai,* ostensibly to treat patients. After meeting Bholanath Sharma and other Congress activists, he became committed to the cause and proved an effective political organizer, making use of his contacts through his medical work and links to other ex-servicemen. He still operated out of Nautanwa, where he became manager of the Congress Party office.

He had previously clashed with local *zamindars,* who were particularly unpopular with the peasants and who had, allegedly, brought in thugs (*goondas*) from India to attack and loot the villages. Singh promised that Congress would now ensure they were punished. Once the Congress armed movement began, the *zamindars* moved their families and moveable property to India and also cooperated with the local Bada Hakim against K. I. Singh and his forces. The struggle was vicious, as the *zamindars* were ill-regarded, and several were killed (Whelpton 2013: 45).

When hostilities against the Ranas started, Singh led a small force of a dozen or so men, with eight or nine rifles, across the border and set up camp at the village of Myudihawa, switching later under pressure from government forces to Karabla, which was more defensible. He managed to obtain additional weapons and food from the local peasantry, and was joined by a combination of peasants, student volunteers and ex-Indian army colleagues –

and, apparently, the Nepal Communist Party and the Rashtriya Mahasabha. He refused to accept 'the Delhi compromise' and ignored Congress' call for a ceasefire. He launched a further attack on Bhairahawa and maintained his rebel base and fighting force. His force had reached about several hundred when he was eventually arrested and jailed in Bhairahawa in February 1951, following a combined operation by the king and the new government – who declared a state of emergency and imposed a curfew in the capital in 23 January 1951, then deployed the army and, with the support of Indian troops (roughly 1000 against 200-400), disarmed and arrested the 'rebels'.

Singh escaped from jail, was re-arrested and sent to Kathmandu. He was released from prison together with two leaders of a Kiranti secessionist movement in January 1952 by mutinying members of the Raksha Dal, a militia composed of former members of the Jana Mukti Sen. Adhikari states that 'the *Kishan Sangh* (peasant organization) led by Singh, allegedly backed by communists, started a peasant revolution demanding implementation of land redistribution in January 1952 and the formation of a party government excluding the *Kukhuri Dal* (knife-wielding gang), pro-Rana reactionaries' (Adhikari 2015: 87). Adhikari also states that 'the members of the Raksha Dal (defence force) occupied the airfield, radio station, post and telephone offices, and even a part of Singha Durbar, where many government officials were oocated. The rebellion was defeated and Singh fled from the country' (Adhkari 2015: 87).

Singh fled to Tibet with some of his supporters, declining the offer to make him leader of the revolt, and the authorities were able to restore control without external intervention by Indian troops. The government then disbanded the Kiranti sections of the Raksha Dal and, on India's suggestion, banned the Communist Party of Nepal and the Rashtriya Mahasabha, which reportedly had taken an active part in the revolt (Adhikari 2015: 86-87. In May 1952, however, agitation developed in the Nautanwa-Bhairahawa area, led by K. I. Singh supporters, who claimed to be influenced by the Chinese communist experience, even if he was still linked to the Nepali Congress.

Singh later returned to Nepal to form the United Democratic Party, possibly with covert funding from the king to help counter what they both felt was the dangerous dominance of the Nepali Congress Party. In 1954, while rallying local farmers, leftist activists launched a planned movement against local feudal landlords at Narikot in Pyuthan (Singh 1992: 25-28). Beginning of January that year, a 3-month training camp was organized under the local Progressive Study Group at Ratmata-Vijayanagar, Pyuthan. Political education and physical training was provided for about 150 local young peasants. The main objective was to train them to fight against landlords and against exploitation. During this movement, agricultural labourers refused to work in the field of landlords for about six months. On the basis of letters written by the area committee, the peasants gather in numbers of between 10,000 and 20,000 within a few hours from all over the district. However, when they took direct action against the landlords in 1957, a brutal police attack led to serious injuries for seven of the agitators, while some 139 were arrested and charged as terrorists and murderers. This put an end to the movement (Karki 2002: 11).

M. B. Singh served briefly as prime minister, appointed by the king, in 1957. Whelpton dubs him a 'royalist Robin Hood', and it seems likely that he did receive support from the king; it seems that Singh saw the possibility of an alliance of the monarchy and the radical forces against the social democratic or centrist Nepali

Congress - much as did the Maoists at certain times during their People's War, as argued by M. B. Singh (Whelpton 2003)[33].

Burman Budhamagar was another early member of the Maoist movement back in the 1950s. In the words of Benoît Cailmail, Budhamagar, 'the leading and most charismatic figure of communism in the village of Thabang in Rolpa' in the early 1990s was also the 'first of the villagers to fight against the local headmen's authority and forms of abuse.' Budhamagar's political career formally began when he joined a farmers' organization in Thabang around 1957. Also at that time, he was active in the Maoist party led by Mohan Bikram Singh. Budhamagar, who was in contact with Singh during his imprisonment for subversive activities, had tried to avoid the ban on the party by opening a front that ostensibly served farmers. Later, Budhamagar also became the Pradhan Panch several times during the Panchayat period. In the first general election of 1959, the people of Thabang gave all their votes to the radical communists, again largely thanks to Budhamagar's influence in the area.

Unrest in the Middle Hills

'A token state presence, the absence of transportation and communication with the outside world, the abundant forest coverage in the Siwalik Hills, and the presence of a large and transient *sukumbasi* population had made the Kamala Valley into ideal terrain for subversive organizing since the 1950s', according to Saubhagya Shah (2018: 50). A local unit of the Communist Party had been set up by Basudev Shrestha in Deuralitar village

33. How far Mahendra himself countenanced this possibility is a moot point, but it is perhaps significant that the king decided in 1956 to re-legalise the Communist Party (banned in 1952 for complicity in the Raksha Dal revolt), and apparently also funded the Marxist-Leninist faction (the Ma Le) which was the continuation of the ultra-radical 'Jhapeli' group.

within a year after the overthrow of the Rana regime in 1950-51[34]. Two years after that, Gananath Koirala and his comrades had begun to organize communist activities in the Kamala Valley and surrounding hill settlements. These activities included expanding the influence of the Communist Party by a combination of 'constructive works' and 'forceful means' (Shah, ibid 53).

The Communist Party was banned in 1951, so much of the work of local cadres like Shrestha and Koirala took place under the banner of the Akhil Nepal Kisan Sangh (the All Nepal Peasants Union). When they began their activities, there were only two schools in the entire district of Sindhuli. Given the demand for education, the communists began teaching pupils in the villages. They made a point of including low-caste 'untouchables' in their schools. 'The schools were a useful way to expand the party organization', commented Shrestha (according to Shah 2018: 53). They also launched a 'ploughing campaign' to encourage men from the higher castes to break the traditional taboo on ploughing; Shah comments that this was 'largely successful' and that by the end of the 1990s 'it was quite normal to see Brahmins and Chhetris ploughing their fields'. The communists failed to break the taboo as far as women were concerned and even now it is taboo for any woman to use the plough; when a few single women tried to do so they were ridiculed and ostracized.

'Forceful actions' included a campaign to reduce the rate of usury to *dasaundi* (ten per cent) from the exorbitant rates (often as high as 60 per cent widely demanded by the money lenders; and the tearing up of records of loans (*tamasuks*) to the poor held by money lenders. They also sometimes organized the collective harvesting by the peasants of thatching materials on hill land

34. Basudev was a relative of Pushpa Lal Shrestha, who founded the Communist Party of Nepal in 18949 in Calcutta. Both men originally came from Ramechhap District.

(*kharphakha*) that was registered to the larger landowners, and their transportation to their villages. 'We were so many, said Basudev, that the owners could never dare oppose us' (Shah 2018: 54).

Unrest in the Eastern Terai

The Terai Congress was founded in 1951 (as the *Terai Newasi Sangh* – Association of Terai People) by Kulanand Jha, Ram Janam Tiwari and Syam Lal Mishra after they failed to get assurances regarding provincial representation in any future Nepal Congress government. Two years later, in 1953, the party claimed 60,000 members and demanded proper representation of the *terai* in the proposed Advisory Assembly. It sought recognition of Hindi as an official language, the establishment of an autonomous *terai* state, and adequate employment of people from the *terai* in the Nepali civil service. In 1954, the leadership passed to Kulanand's brother, Vedananda Jha, who was appointed as Minister of Home Affairs, Development, Industry and Commerce in 1961 and later (in 1977) became Ambassador to India.

In early 1952, there was a revolt by poor and landless peasants in Rautahat and a movement to destroy loan contract papers drawn up to legitimize high interest loans made by money-lenders and large landowners to these people. Known as the *Tamsuk Fatta Andolan* (the bondage paper destruction movement), its attacks were directed not only at those individuals considered to be guilty personally but also at district land registration offices where the records and land mortgage papers (*bhog bandagi*) that were often used as security against the loans were held (Kishan Sangharsha 1977: 30). The movement was crushed, with numerous people being injured and with arrests and detentions made by the police (Karki 2002: 10).

Despite – or perhaps even because – of state repression, this was followed in 1952-53, by a movement in Rautahat and Bara which struggled not just for land and other rights, but for dignity and social respect. It was called: *re nahi, ji kaho andolan* – The Say 'Hello', not 'Hey you' Movement – and protested against the use of disrespectful and humiliating language by landlords and by the bullying of peasants and landless labourers. According to Karki (2002: 10), 'it played an important role in the history of peasant movements in Nepal and had an influence on subsequent movements'. In Birgunj, where there was a procession with slogans, five were killed and 125 injured; in Rautahat, Asarfi Saha was murdered in 1953. The peasants involved also adopted the slogan '*maddat bhakari, khada karo*', and helped each other to save and store grain in support of their struggle (INSEC 1995: 158, cited by Basnet 2008: 25).

In Bara and Rautahat, the peasant movements were also focused on *dharma bhakari* – best described as 'a food grain fund', which involves local contributions and is made available to those in need either at the beginning of the agricultural season or during the 'hungry period'. It is not entirely clear what the issue was, but the movement in both districts was referred to as *dharma bhakari andolan* (the *dharma bhakari* movement).

At the beginning of 1953, there was a rally of the All Nepal Peasants Association (ANPA) in Bara, calling for the land of the big landowners and big *birta* holders to be confiscated and distributed to middle and small farmers and landless people. It called also for an end to exploitation of small farmers and landless people by feudal landlords. The landowners rallied to suppress the movement. According to the ANPA chairman, Keshav Badal, 1,000 kg of rice was cooked at each mealtime for the participating peasants. This huge gathering of protestors was attacked by armed police under the regional administrator on 22 January 1953 to arrest the peasant leaders: Madhu Singh, Comrade Ran Vriksya Chaudhari, Nanda Kishwar Chaudhari, Mohan Singh Mahato, Nandan Aryal, Dev Narayan Kalwar, Ram Lal Tharu, Rama Kanta and Nathuni. During the struggle, 19 year old Mukha Lal Mahato was killed by police fire. Others were arrested and tortured; and the movement was suppressed (Karki 2002: 11).

On 15 May 1953, the Nepali Congress Party launched a 'no-rent' campaign in the eastern *terai* at Biratnagar where B P Koirala addressed a crowd of 35,000 people asking them to defy the government's 'lock-out' order regarding Biratnagar Jute Mill. During the first week of June, the movement spread to the Birgunj, Biratnagar, Saptari, Janakpur, Mahottari area. Ram Narayan Mishra along with Saroj Koirala toured the region organizing peasant meetings and asking them not to pay their land rent.

The first congress of the All Nepal Peasants Association was held in Rautahat in 1954. It elected Tulsi Lal Amatya as president, Ram Hari Sharma as vice-president, Shamburam Shrestha and Niranjan Govind Vaidhya as general secretary and secretary respectively. The executive Committee consisted of 23 members. The second congress was held in Janakpur in 1956. Tulsi Lal Amarya was again elected president with D P Sharma and Shamburam Shrestha as vice-president and general secretary respectively. This time the executive committee comprised 31 members (Dhakal 2013: 133 footnote 1).

Basnet suggests that 'from 1953 to 1955 in almost all districts of the *terai*, '*khamar rok*' – a form of farmers' movement – took place, which was controlled and led by young farmers (Thapa 2001)' (Basnet 2008: 26). It was in the eastern *terai*, however, that most of the action was concentrated. Between 1953 and 1956 there was a movement which started in Jhapa and moved to other regions of the *terai*, called *khamar roko* or *khamar rok* (Abolish

Owner's Private Property), which seems to have been influenced by communists in Bengal. Khamar in Bengali means *nij-jote* land, which is equivalent to *jirayat* land. In 1955-56, a movement in Siraha resulted in the death of Bahadur Saha. Between 1956 and 1958, there was a peasant movement in Saptari, in which Aghori Yadav was killed. The government formed 'a small reformist commission' in response to this unrest, but this did not represent the tenants or landless peasants in any way (Basnet 2008: 26).

Land Reform and Rural Unrest

Initial moves towards land reform began with the Land and Cultivation Record Compilation Act of 1956, and continued with the Land Acts of 1957, when the government began to compile a register of tenants and tenancies. In the absence of a full and comprehensive land register, however, the impact of this legislation remained limited. During the 1959 general election, the Nepali Congress Party introduced the slogan: '*jamin jotneko; ghar potneko*' (land to the tillers and houses to those who 'smear' them (INSEC 1995: 155-164). The slogan became very popular among poor peasants and landless people, helping the Congress Party to win a majority of the parliamentary seats.

One of the key policies of the first elected government of Nepal in 1959 was land reform. As Sugden has noted, 'given the importance of agriculture in Nepal and the failure of agriculture to meet the needs of the population, reforms were seen as a first step to improve the conditions of the peasantry and it became an important political agenda' (Alden-Wily et al 2008; Regmi 1976; Sugden). *Birta* estates were nationalised in 1959 by the Birta Abolition Act and many tenant farmers benefited as a result, acquiring title to the land they had settled and farmed. This was supported by the US in particular, with Wolf Ladejinsky a key advisor to several Asian governments (including Japan, Taiwan,

India and Nepal) and perhaps the most influential advocate of using agrarian reforms to win the support of the peasantry in order to pre-empt communist appeals by 'stealing communist thunder', in one of his memorable formulations.

Such measures were seen, however, as a threat by some: 'the land reforms – *birta* abolition and revision in tenancy laws – enacted by the Nepali Congress government disturbed the position of the landed aristocracy, which was also a dominant factor in the military. The weakening position of landlords, bureaucracy and military meant the weakening of that of the king' and, as Adhikari comments, 'the landowners with vested interests – Ranas, *zamindars,* etc. – started to prepare for civil war to defeat the reform measures undertkane by the government. They began resorting to indiscriminate exploitation of the peasants and evicted them from their lands. Thus, the clash between the landlords and peasants began: peasants started revolting and the feudals took recourse to violence and widespread lawlessness' (Adhikari 2015: 91 and 90).

There were also reactionary movements from below, encouraged by religious fundamentalists. For example, a *yogi* Naraharinath of the Karmavir Mahamandal – an ultra-right party – and his followers began to spread a baseless rumour among the people in Gorkha that the NC government intended to confiscate their property, impose taxes on personal (property) such as heads of goats and tails of pigs, and so on. Declaring himself a reincarnation of Saint Goraknath, he exhorted the people to rise up in arms against a 'sinful' government. This led to cases of looting and murder until the government was forced to send in the army to suppress the revolt (Adhikari 2015: 90).

8

Rural Unrest in the 1960s

Land Reform and Resistance

When King Mahendra dissolved the multi-party system that had been in place during the 1950s, in favour of a party-less Panchayat Democracy, all political parties were banned and their leaders threatened with imprisonment. The communists officially moved to India, first to Darbhanga in Bihar, then in Varanasi from 1961 to 1974, and finally to Gorakhpur; but the activists remained inside the country, operating underground, holding meetings, distributing pamphlets and even leading or participating in a few demonstrations. The All Nepal Peasants Association (ANPA) was banned, as indeed were all peasant associations, and a state-sponsored 'Nepal Peasants' Organisation' was established to 'represent' the interests of small farmers.

On the advice of the US (among others), but also to some extent of his own volition as a part of a process of modernization and development (*vikas*), Mahendra initiated various programmes of rural development. and one of the most significant attempts at far-reaching land reform was made with the Lands Act in 1964 – a government initiative whose significance has been much debated over the years (see Adhikari 2008), but which undoubtedly gave an impetus to increased rural unrest. There were also isolated events of violence, as when Durgananda Jha threw a bomb at King Mahendra in 1961 – an act for which he was executed under a law that was hastily introduced with retrospective effect. But there were also more organized land rights and peasant movements, some of which were a direct response to government initiatives, ad some of which were a response to the lack of government initiatives.

When King Mahendra took power in 1961, he retained a commitment to land reform as a key element in his strategy for development in Nepal, and as a way of legitimizing his new 'partyless panchayat regime'. The Agricultural Reorganization Act, which was passed in 1963, and the Land Reform Act of 1964 imposed a ceiling on private land holdings and proposed to redistribute the expropriated surplus land to tenant farmers. It also aimed at increasing the security of tenure of tenant farmers. It had some effect on the size of landholdings and clarified tenure arragements to a significant degree.

The official land ceiling – 25 *bighas* (17 hectares) in the *terai* and inner *terai*, 50 *ropani* (2.5 hectares) in the Kathmandu Valley and 80 *ropani* (4 hectares) in the hills and mountains - was not in reality imposed, in part because landowners were able to re-assign land holdings to family members or to falsify the record, and but also in part because the administration lacked both the political will and the resources to implement the reforms. The government had reportedly acquired around 50,000 hectares by 1972. But Regmi (1976) noted that this constituted only about 3 per cent of the cultivable area and it was estimated (according to Alden-Wily et al 2008) that only 22,000 hectares were actually redistributed, benefiting just 10,000 small farmers. Land ceilings were weakly enforced, little land was redistributed and landlords rather than tenants often gained from the new rules.

In reality, significant land holdings were sold off or distributed to relatives and others by larger landowners concerned by the implications of the Land Reform Act and the possibility of confiscation. Frederick Gaige provides a case study from northern Kapilvastu in the western *terai* which illustrates this point (Gaige 1975: 75). The land sales did contribute to a certain redistribution of landowership, but other mechanisms were used to maintain a high degree of concentration of land ownership (Adhikari 2006, 2011; Alden-Wily et al 2008; Deuja 2008). Joshi aand Mason (2007: 404) estimated that, after the reforms of the 1960s, some 3 per cent of households in Nepal still owned about 27 per cent of arable land, while 62 per cent of 'peasant' households owned less than half (49 per cent).

Neither the 1964 Land Act nor the 1964 Land Rules stated specifically that a tenant required a citizenship certificate before purchasing or otherwise acquiring land; but in article 3 of section 3 of the Rules, tenants were required to provide details of their citizenship. This created considerable problems for many tenants, especially those in the western *terai* (Kapilvastu, Rupandehi and Nawal Parasi) where the *ukhada* system – under which Indian *zamindars* had been given title to large landholdings which they tended to parcel out to tenants (also mostly Indians) - was widespread. Few of these tenants acquired citizenship between 1952, when it was first possible to do so, and 1964, when the land reform programme was initiated. Under the Land Act, tenants were entitled to a maximum of 4 *bighas* (2.7 hectares) for cultivation only (Sugden & Gurung 2012).

The Ukhada Land Tenure Act of 1964 stated that title to Ukhada lands in excess of landholding ceilings should be transferred from *zamindars* to tenants, unless the tenants were proven to be aliens. This effectively encouraged the *zamindars* to identify their tenants as aliens, as they were then able either to sell any excess land or to transfer title to others (including relatives), while making informal arrangements to retain de facto control. As Gaige remarks, 'thus, the law and the accompanying rules perpetuated the economic and social status quo by encouraging a kind of class struggle in which the government legitimized the landowners' interests' (1975: 96). Under the 1964 rules, the tenants would simply have remained tenants, but the Ukhada Land Tenure First Amendment Act of 1965, introduced ostensibly to alleviate potential landowner-tenant conflict, actually made things worse for the tenants.

This amendment stated that 'in case such peasant is, or is subsequently proved to be, an alien, the *ukhada* lands cultivated by him shall be registered in the name of His Majesty's Government, which may sell or distribute such lands to landless Nepalese peasants on any condition' (Gaige 1975: 97). This placed tenants in the areas of the *terai* affected by the reforms in an even more precarious position – they were now effectively threatened with dispossession. It was now to the landowner's advantage to evict his tenants and cultivate as much of his holding as possible himself, and the tenant risked dispossession an eviction as an alien, to be replaced by re-settled 'Nepali' peasants, who were most likely to be incomers from the hills.

For by this time, the *terai* was becoming an increasingly attractive place for small farmers in the densely populated and arguably over-crowded hill areas to relocate to, given the availability of land for cultivation and the improvements in conditions there. The *terai* had long been considered unhealthy – hot, malarial - and unwelcoming. But during the latter part of the 1950s and early 1960s, a malaria eradication programme sponsored by the USA and WHO proved very effective in significantly reducing the incidence of malaria in the *terai*. Consequently, there was rapid growth during the 1960s and 1970s in the scale of immigration of would-be settlers (*sukumbasi*) into the *terai*, both from the hill areas to the north (in Nepal) and also from the plains to the south (in India).

The combination of the 'opening up' of the *terai* and the pressure for land reform led to a significant transformation of land settlement, occupation and tenure across the region. This, in turn, was associated with the land dispossession of some indigenous groups and by land acquisition by other groups, some indigenous but most incomers from the north and the south.

Unrest in the Western Terai

In 1960, according to Basnet (2008: 26), in 1960, a historical farmers' struggle took place in the district of Dang, for which the seeds were sown in the election of 1958 (INSEC 1995). In that election, the slogans of the Nepali Congress Party (*'jagga kasko? jotneko!' and 'ghar kasko? potneko!*) fueled the movement. A peasant uprising took place in Beluwa-Banjadi in Dang Deukhuri in 1961. As a result, the landlords in the area began to deprive substantial numbers of tenants, who had been cultivating the land on condition of assured tenancy rights, of their entitlement. Instead, they attempted to impose sharecropping arrangements giving themselves rights to 50 per cent or even in some cases two-thirds of the harvest.

In response to this, peasants from Gairagaon, Gulariya, Ratanpur, Beluwa-Banjadi and Karjahi village development committees organized themselves to resist the landowners' initiative. They were aided by Communist Party activists Narayan Prasad Sharma, Ram Prasad Devkota, Manik Lal Gautam and Keshav Raj Gautam. On 31 January 1961, the landlords recruited hired thugs to attempt to seize the mustard crop from the threshing grounds of the peasants of Beluwa-Banjadi. A serious clash resulted, during which the peasants managed to capture some of the hired men and handed them over to the local administration. According to the local ANPA leaders, the landlords made no further attempts to seize the peasants' crops (Karki 2010: 11).

In 1967, 148 Tharu families, led by Chilla Tharu, settled in what was locally known as the Kanara jungle, most of them from Dang. The Kanara jungle lies on the western bank of the Babai River and east of Dhodari village. It is about half an hour's walk from Gulariya, the headquarters of Bardiya District to the north and Padnaha village to the south. It had been cleared in the late 1940s (maybe in 1946) by a Brahmin landowner named Hakim Baje, using his *kamaiyas;* but the area was abandoned after a few years because of attacks by wild animals and the Kanara settlement returned to the jungle.

Now, 20 years later, a well dug for drinking water and a couple of *bar-pipal* (banyan) trees were found as remnants of this earlier settlement. The *sukumbasi* collected timber from the surrounding forest to build huts and used wood from the forest for fuel. They also collected fodder for their livestock and used waste land to build shelter for their animals. Even more importantly, as Dhakal remarks, 'the advantage of proximity to forest areas lies in the fact that it could provide to collect tubers, roots, shoots, berries and other edible fruits, which provided supplementary and nutritious food. The Babai River on the eastern border of the settlement formed a water source. They could irrigate their land and also fish in the river, a traditional activity of the Tharus' (2013: 142). The *sukumbasi* were, however, forcefully evicted by the government, following complaints by local landowners, and some were jailed.

Unrest in the West Central terai

In the years immediately following the Land (Reform) Act of 1964, there was a rush of title transfers in many parts of the *terai* as landowners tried to devolve themselves of official ownership. In many cases, tenants and sharecroppers were replaced by cultivators in whose name the land was registered, but who remained effectively subordinate to the original landowner;

in other cases, *ukhada* tenants were replaced by daily wage labourers. This latter tendency was particularly prevalent in the western *terai.*

September 1966, a crowd, estimated around 4,000 surrounded the Nawal Parasi district administrative office in Parasi in response to fears (and the reality) of such changes (Seddon 1984: 148). Local security forces opened fire, killing some and injuring more (the official figures were nine and 12 respectively). No proper investigation was ever carried out, but an official report stated that the local people had rioted and threatened the lives of officials. Although this was clearly a local peasant demonstration, linked to the denial of land rights and 'legal' actions initiated by local landowners and the local authorities against small-holders and tenants, it was labelled by the Kathmandu media, notably the state controlled *Gorkhapatra,* as having been instigated by 'certain elements' who had 'misguided the peasants on the issue of land reform' and who should 'not be left unpunished'. These 'elements' were allegedly linked to India.

There was another shooting incident in Nawalparasi after the car of the assistant Minister of Education was stoned and the chief district officer attacked, as police fired on the crowd and four people were injured. Some 'egregiously offensive local officials were removed and arrested students were released as in Kathmandu', but 'firm suppression of people was applied at a relatively early stage, with the army sent down to control the border and to suppress the agitation. Police were given 'shoot at sight' orders to suppress the agitations' (Sah ibid: 286).

According to the blueprint of the compulsory savings scheme initiated by the government in 1965, every farmer was required to deposit a small percentage of his crop with the government each year. This was viewed by most farmers as an additional tax, despite the government's promise to return the deposit with interest at the end of a five year period. Many of the larger landowners were able to avoid making these compulsory savings; but small farmers and peasants were less able to resist or refuse, and savings were often collected using various means of coercion or intimidation from those least able to afford to give up any portion of their income. Over the next few years, there were also constant reports in the press suggesting that the officials concerned were not keeping adequate records of the amounts 'saved' in this way and that the farmers' savings were being, in effect, misappropriated.

Resistance to payment gradually increased, and in April 1969 broke out in Taulihawa, the capital of Kapilvastu District when a crowd of women surrounded and attacked officials attempting to collect compulsory savings. Violence quickly spread across Kapilvastu District and into the adjacent Rupandehi District. Compulsory-savings deposits were broken into a looted and burned. The police responded, often violently with shooting at protestors and looters in some thirty villages over a three-week period, as a result of which some 33 people died, hundreds were injured and many others arrested. The movement forced the government to suspend the scheme for compulsory savings throughout the country.

Unrest in Eastern Nepal

In Sindhuli, when the process of land alienation became too severe in the 1960s, the government enforced an administrative measure to control the sale of land from the indigenous Majhis and Danuwars to the new immigrants. Large-scale land transfers tended to impoverish those who had lived in the area, as hunters, gatherers and fisherfolk for possibly centuries, living off 'the land' and local natural resources but without any formal system of landholding. Many of the immigrants were either prevented by the local authorities from settling or else, when settled unofficially, were evicted by force if needs be. As these 'illegal' settlers often ignored the eviction notices posted by officials, the Forest Department would employ a large number of forest guards and policemen, often with elephants, to chase the settlers from the land, and to dismantle and sometimes burn their dwellings.

According to local informants, the first eviction in Viman took place around 1969. 'The evicted squatters were given the option of moving to the far western *terai* region where the government had launched several re-settlement projects that gave landless peasant families four *bighas* of land and other services to start anew. Several dozen families from Viman accepted the government's offer and moved to western Nepal, but others chose to stay on in the valley' (Shah 2018: 48).

But, as Shah remarks, 'in a manner reminiscent of 'every day forms of peasant resistance' delineated by James Scott, the squatters responded by organizing to wear down the will of a weak state to keep them out of the forest land. Working as a group, the squatters would either re-occupy the area or move to a new forest after the eviction team had left the area' (2018: 49). The government's cumbersome and episodic measures were no match for the dogged persistent of the *sukumbasis* who were often aided by local politicians. As the contest over land became more heated, the squatter issue became firmly linked with the underground communist politics of the Kamala Valley.

Divisions within the Communist Movement

After King Mahendra's coup, when all political parties were banned, the Communist Party moved to India – first, to Darbhanga in Bihar, then to Vanarasi from 1961 to 1974, and finally to Gorakhpur – but many activists remained inside Nepal and continued the struggle underground. In 1961, when the party divided into different tendencies or factions, K I Singh rallied the leftist groups, demanding a Constituent Assembly. This received considerable support amongst the party grassroots, but he did not get much support from fellow Central Committee members. When the party eventually split in 1962, Singh sided with the more radical Communist Party led by Tulsi Lal Amatya and maintained a revolutionary commitment to popular mobilisation and armed struggle 'when the time was ripe' throughout his subsequent political career.

In 1962, at the Third Party Congress, the Communist Party of Nepal divided effectively into a pro-Soviet and a pro-China faction. In 1968, Pushpa Lal, the founder of the Communist Party of Nepal (CPN), also left the main body of the Communist Party of Nepal (Tulsi Lal Group). to establish a separate group, which became known as the CPN (Pushpa Lal). More communist groupings developed from this original split. In 1971, a group of CPN leaders — Manmohan Adhikari, Sambhu Ram Shrestha, and Mohan Bikram Singh — were released from jail and together formed the Central Nucleus, which tried to unite with Pushpa Lal's group. This failed, because of Pushpa Lal's objective of uniting all the democratic forces, including the Nepali Congress, against the Panchayat Regime, and Central Nucleus itself broke apart[35].

35. Adhikari formed the Communist Party of Nepal (Manmohan), which developed close relations with the Communist Party of India (Marxist); M. B. Singh and Nirma Lal founded what became known as Communist Party of Nepal (4th Congress) after the Fourth Party Congress held in September 1974; other splinter groups included the Nepal Workers and Peasants Party, the Communist Party of Nepal (Krishna Das), the Communist Party of Nepal (Burma), and the Communist Party of Nepal (Manandhar). In 1975, Pushpa Lal's group developed into the Communist Party of Nepal (Marxist-Leninist) and the original CPN became just one of many factions, eventually taking the name CPN (Amatya) and adopting a pro-Soviet position.

9

Rural Unrest the 1970s

Rural unrest continued throughout the 1970s. As Suresh Dakhal remarked, 'during the 70s also, peasant movements were occurring in several parts of the country, especially in the western *terai*. These included places such as Dang, Nawalparasi, Kapilvastu and Palpa'. 'Similarly, places like Jugedi in Chitwan, Dhanusha in Janakpur, Chula Chuli in Ilam and Dhankuta in the east also saw such movements' (Dhakal 2013: 133-34).

Unrest in the Eastern Terai

In 1970, what started as a local struggle by settlers (*sukumbasi*) in the area of Biratnagar to occupy an area of forest land (known, ironically, as *ramailo jhoda* or 'lovely Jhoda'), intensified and began to spread. In January 1971, the army encircled and opened fire on landless settlers who were clearing land in the forest in various parts of Morang District – in Kanepokhari, Pathari, Dahijhoda, Jarayotar, Bayarban, Jadaha, Bhaunne and Chisang. The *sukumbasis* were defenceless against the bullets of the army; those killed were allegedly loaded onto trucks and later thrown into the Koshi River. There was a national protest by *sukumbasi,* supported by the banned political parties in outrage against the killing. As a result of this, the government introduced the Jhoda Land Act 2028 (1971) which guaranteed land rights to landless people up to a maximum of four *bighas* per family. This Act has, however, never been fully implemented.

According to Karki, another military operation in 1976 displaced the *sukumbasi* from Jhoda, situated to the south of Chulachuli and to the north of the East-West Highway. Again, in 1983, the entire village of Chulachuli was displaced, following a declaration that the land was to be used for re-forestation. On 8 January 1985, as many as 2,400 men and women marched towards Bahragoth, Chulachuli, carrying photos of the King and Queen; they were *lathi*-charged by some 400-500 police near the Ratuwa Bridge on the East-West Highway. Many protestors, including women, sustained serious injuries. The issue of Chulachuli remained unresolved throughout the Panchayat period (Singh 1992: 338-353, cited in Karki 2002: 12).

In 1971, under the influence of the teachings of Mao Tse Tung and the experience of Charu Mazumdar, architect of the Naxalite uprising in Bihar and elsewhere in India, a group of young communist party activists – including K. P. Oli, Radha Krishna Mainali and Chandra Prakah Mainali - formed the Koshi Regional Committee of the CPN, in Jhapa. These young activists launched an underground guerrilla movement, popularly known as 'the Jhapa uprising', in line with the Maoist concept of a protracted People's War. Pandey and Rimal draw attention to the fact that several women were closely involved in the 'Jhapa Bidroha', including Sharada Mainali, Lila Kattel, Gaura Prasain and Sita Khadka, providing shelter to the underground leaders and 'exchanging news and information'; three of these women served jail terms as a result (Pandey & Rimal nd: 17).

The movement actually started in Jymirgadi village in Jhapa on 16 May 1971 and attracted the attention and support of many young activists across the country. It was directed mainly against the large 'semi-feudal' landowners and led to the killing of eight landlords. The movement was brought to a swift end by a brutal counter-insurgency campaign by the police, which led to hundreds of its followers being killed, jailed or forced into exile. Five leaders of the movement - Ramnath Dahal, Netra Ghimire, Biren Rajbanshi, Krishna Kuinkel and Narayan Shrestha - who were subsequently executed (on – variously – 24 February or 4 March 1973) by firing squad in a wooded area in Sukhani, Ilam after being taken there from Chandagadhi, Jhapa under the pretext of shifting them to another prison (Karki 2002: 12). K. P. Oli was also arrested, was released shortly but was then again arrested and charged with treason. He spent 14 consecutive years in jail until 1987[36].

Despite the crushing of the movement, members of the group continued to conduct clandestine political work amongst the peasants of Jhapa and, in 1975, the survivors of the Jhapa movement took the initiative to found the All Nepal Communist Revolutionary Coordination Committee (Marxist-Leninist). Other small groups merged with ANCRCC (ML) and, on 26 December 1978, ANCRCC (ML) organized the founding congress of the Communist Party of Nepal (Marxist-Leninist). C. P. Mainali was elected general secretary of the party. CPN (ML) – known as Ma-Le - was an underground party, and during 1979 conducted small-scale, armed operations against the regime and feudal landlords, with a view to eventually initiating 'an agrarian uprising' or armed revolt (according to Deepak Thapa (2001), cited in Karki & Seddon 2003: 12).

The tactics of armed struggle, however, did not prove particularly successful, and the party changed its political approach, and started to focus more on mobilizing mass movements for a democratic change. Mainali, clearly identified

---

36. In March 2017, now Chairman of the CPN-UML, he led a 15-day campaign which included a visit to Sukhani Park where tributes were offered to 'the martyrs' of the Jhapa uprising, to officially launch the nationwide campaign.

with the initial militant phase of the party, was removed from his post of general secretary and replaced by Jhala Nath Khanal. Subsequently, according to Mikesell, 'abandoned the people's war for underground educating and organizing in village, town, school and campus in order to build a mass movement' (Mikesell 1999: 100). The Party united with a number of other communist party factions in the early 1990s to form the Communist Party (United Marxist-Leninist) or UML.

In the meanwhile, as the communists struggled to come to terms with the Jhapa experience and the implications of the rise of Maoism, some sections of the Nepali Congress Party continued the armed struggle. But they tended to rely on 'terrorism' rather than mass movements of local peasants. There were bombings in Haripur in Saptari district in August 1972, and in Biratnagar and Malangawa in December 1973; there was a passenger plane hijacking in June 1973 and a failed attempt to assassinate King Birendra by a bomb attack in Birtnagar in March 1974, and another bomb attack against Prayagraj Singh Suwal in May 1974. In December 1974, the government received intelligence that 'many revolutionaries were planning to capture Okhaldhunga'. The army was sent to intervene and they suppressed an incipient insurgency, killing some of those involved, including Ram, Laxman and other youths. Captain Yagya Bahadur Thapa and Bhim Narayan Shrestha were captured and given death sentences. This incident is known as 'the Timburbote Incident'.

Unrest in the Western and Central Hills

A local movement began in Barre, in Argha Khanchi District in 1974, when, under the leadership of Keshar Mani Pokharel, local peasants launched an initiative to seize property from the local landlords. The government's response to this movement, known as 'the Barre Movement', was rapid and effective. The movement was quickly suppressed (Adhikari 2008: 32; Rawal 1990: 70).

In January 1975, Narayan Man Bijukche (known as 'Comrade Rohit') formed the Nepal Workers and Peasants Party (NMKP), a communist party with an explicit commitment to the peasantry, which has retained a strong base in Bhaktapur. It was initially a break-away from the Communist Party of Nepal led by Pushpa Lal, and an amalgamation of the Proletarian Revolutionary Organisation, Nepal and the Kisan Samiti (which may have been linked with the earlier Akhil Nepal Kishan Sangh). Over the years, this party has retained a considerable following in Bhaktapur, but has failed to extend its influence much beyond this limited arena, despite its all-embracing name and presumably wider ambitions.

According to Adhikari (2008: 32), another outbreak of peasant unrest occurred in 1978 in Piskar village in Sindhupalchowk District when poor peasants, who were mainly Thami people, seized rice from the granaries of local landlords. The landlords called in the police to suppress the unrest, and two people were killed. Others suffered as they were forced to flee their village (Adhikari 2008: 32). Basnet also refers to what he calls the 'Piskor movement' that he says arose in Sindhupalchowk in 1983. This was directed primarily against the Pandeys of Piskor (Piskar) village. Peasants had been obliged to provide free labour services to these Pandeys, pay high rates of interest on loans contracted with them, and had to hand over 'most of their production' to the landlords (Basnet 2008: 27). They organized themselves and demanded '*jasko jot usko pot*' – land to the tillers (ANPA 2004, cited in Basnet 2008: 27). But the movement was crushed and several poor peasants and landless people were killed[37].

37. It seems as though these two accounts relate to the same incident, but further research is needed to be sure.

Unrest in the West Central Terai

In 1977, there was a local movement to seize the property of landlords in Jugedi, in Chitwan District. It was suppressed by the police (Adhikari 2008: 32).

In May 1979, some 500 *sukumbasis,* who were squatting on public land, assembled in Barghat in Nawalparasi District and surrounded the local police station to protest against the detention of some of their fellow settlers, the seizure of their farm implements and other property. They had previously requested the local *panchas* (village council chairmen), the Chief District Officer and a minister to tour the district and learn for themselves how far the local people were being intimidated and harassed by the forest guards and the local police, and asked that they be accorded their legal title to land. According to Krishna Ghimire (1992: 144), 'the official response to the *sukumbasis* and their demands was immediate repression... the police opened fire without warning'. Hundreds were injured.

Unrest in the Central Eastern Hills

In the Kamal Valley in Sindhuli District, the active presence of the communist party was, as we have seen, was a major feature of the region from the early 1950s onwards. When King Mahendra banned the political parties and introduced the party-less Panchayat system, Basudev Shrestha joined the establishment, and was elected to the Rastriya Panchayat (National Assembly). With the departure of their former leader, new cadres took over. Rishi Devkota and C. P. Gajurel took charge of the communist party in Sindhuli. The approach of these new leaders was more radical, and they aligned themselves very much with the Fourth Convention, the faction of the communist party headed by Mohan Bikram Singh and Nirmal Lama, and espoused a harder line (*ugra baam*).

Private granaries began to be confiscated by communist party cadres, under their inspiration and guidance; in some places, like Kauche village, collective farming was practiced. 'Educational' or indoctrination classes were held in various places, including Kauche – which was considered a 'hot-bed' of communist activity even by the standards of the Kamala Valley - and those who opposed the Party's programmes was considered to be 'anti-social', 'corrupt', 'immoral' or even as 'exploiters' and thus as class enemies. Shah cites a local who refers to the way in which his uncle – a long time communist party worker – was tortured because he differed from the party 'line' on doubling the minimum wage, and argues that 'the communists began to rely on increasingly harsh measures to implement their programmes and to silence dissent' (2018: 55). He suggests that 'the logical progression of the ultra-left path culminated in the assassination of Raghunath Koirala in 1979. The sensational killing provoked an equally swift and ruthless response from the state against the Communist Party in the Kamala Valley' (2018: 55).

The Party weathered the storm and began to adopt more moderate means to maintain its hold in the district', but, after his murder, Raghunath Koirala's family joined the Nepali Congress Party, despite the fact that his elder brother, Ghananath, had been the first communist leader in the Viman area. The local whose uncle was tortured also stated that his whole family 'quit the communists and sided with the Nepali Congress after what happened to their uncle' (2018: 56). Clearly, the Nepali Congress was seen to offer an alternative to the communists or those disillusioned with communist party theory and practice, but despite increasing support for it during this period as a result of 'communist excesses', it was never able to offer a party network as pervasive and influential as that of the communists in Sindhuli.

Unrest in the Eastern Hills

In the winter of 1979, in Chintang, in the Khalsa area of Dhankuta District in the eastern hills, there was a local uprising of peasants, mainly Rais, against local landlords (the *majhiyas)* and authorities, also mainly Rais. This was a classic example of the situation Whelpton described as one form of political conflict in which 'tensions between the peasantry and those claiming a share of their produce as rent or taxation could result in violence and, where both cultivator and landlord were from the same ethnic group, this could be seen as straightforward class conflict'.

There was a long history of leftist political organization in the area, from the 1950s onwards. In the mid-1960s, Mohan Chandra Adhikari had come to the Khalsa area as a school teacher in Chungbaang, and in 1967, he formed a Khalsa Area Committee as a branch of the CPN-Marxist. The members of the committee were active in promoting concern among the local peasantry regarding the dominance of the *majhiyas* in Chintang and surrounding areas of Khalsa. A *majhiya* was in effect a local form of *jimindar,* as the *majhiyas* were appointed as village representatives to collect land taxes and were able to call on local labour to cultivate their own fields on land that was tax-exempt. They also had links to higher level authorities. Rather than being representatives of their community, however, they acted more as state functionaries and as owners rather than custodians of the land although they claimed they were *kipatiya (kipat* holders). In fact, however, land tenure in Khalsa did not share the *kipat* system characteristic of much of the eastern hills, as it was not communally but privately owned.

The Khalsa area comprised mainly hilly rain-fed *bari* land, suitable for millet, maize and legumes; rice production was undertaken only by a small number of farmers in the lowlands.

Land distribution was very unequal and many small farmers were also share-croppers, agricultural labourers and porters. Most suffered from food shortages and maintained close serf-like relations with the larger landlords to enable them to borrow food grain during the 'hungry season'; this meant sometimes that they were obliged to provide free labour (*jhara*) to these landlords (the *majhiyas*) during peak agricultural seasons, and on special occasions.

In 1970-71, two young men, Govind Bikal and Bam Devan, had arrived in the village as school teachers[38]. The two young men had links with communists in Dharan, where they came from, and had been influenced by the Jhapa uprising and the Indian Naxalites. They set up a library at the school, giving it the name of Lali Guras Pustakalaya (Rhododendron Library); they collected 'progressive' literature (including the works of Mao Tse Tung) and the library became a centre for local youth, particularly for the discontented. They and other local activists maintained close links with the Party in Dharan, but the library now became a training centre for the Purba Koshi Prantiya Committee, another faction of the communist party. Also, Man Mohan Adhikari, who was now leading yet another communist faction party faction which had split from Mohan Bikram Singh's 'Nucleus', came with other comrades to visit Chintang to train their cadres and establish a party committee.

It seems that there was a serious drought in 1970-71, local food production had collapsed, and many families were starving. The granaries in the *majhiya* households, however, were full. A 'movement' broke out to 'borrow' grain from these rich households; apparently old women were involved (Adhikari

38. The school itself had been founded in 1951 by Bishnumaya Majhiya and had received financial support, among others from Suyra Bahadur Thapa in the mid-1960s.

2008: 32). It was not exactly a seizure, and those 'borrowing' the grain even provided receipts; but it was effectively forced on the dominant *majhiya* households who, not surprisingly, took exception to this action. Some of them filed a complaint against those whom they identified as the instigators, which included Bikal, Devan and other activists, and some of the peasants taking the 'loans', accusing them of theft. The CDO heard the charges and many were arrested and jailed for six months. Many of them were ill-treated while in detention. They fought their cases, however, and the courts eventually upheld their claims that these had been 'forced loans' rather than theft.

Unrest in the Eastern Terai

On 6 April 1979, students demonstrated in Kathmandu against the execution of former Prime Minister of Pakistan Zulfikar Ali Bhutto, but as the crowd approached the Pakistani embassy, they were stopped by police at Lainchaur. In the following days there was student agitation related to this incident at several colleges in the eastern *terai*. But although this started with students, things soon took a different turn and became more widespread. Student protests were soon overshadowed by those by factory workers and by farmers opposed to higher land taxes, and more generally by those responding to corruption and mal-administration. The main centre for this was Janakpur, where the chief district officer and the zonal commissioner were both subsequently suspended.

At the beginning of 1978 (or alternatively in 1979-80), there was a peasant uprising in the vicinity of Janakpur in Dhanusha District, when poor peasants and landless labourers launched a movement called *bhakari phor andolan* (Break the Granary Movement), which, among other things, took over the granary of Justice Prakash Man in Dhanusha. But this was relatively short-lived, and was rapidly suppressed by the army (Karki

2002: 13; Adhikari 2008: 32). Alternatively, the struggle started in Dhanusha but spread to different parts of the country (Thapa 2001, cited in Basnet 2008: 27).

In May 1979, a variety of protests broke out, again mainly in the area of Janakpur, and there were major clashes which led to the deaths of five people (one policeman and four demonstrators), according to government reports. A Home Ministry report released on 19 May indicated serious disturbances in four separate incidents in Dhanusha district, in Siraha and in places west of Janakpur. The report spoke of 'a series of mob attacks' on customs posts and government warehouses (*godowns*), involving the burning of some buildings, direct attacks on government officials, and attempts to disrupt traffic along the East West Highway.

On 20 May, it was reported the demonstrators had removed portraits of the King and Queen from office and that they had been burned in effigy. The railway terminus at Janakpur was also set on fire, putting Nepal's only rail service out of operation. The independent daily, Motherland, carried a Home Ministry report saying that six people were killed when police fired on a crowd between Janakpur and Birgunj, in Sirlahi District. The next day, although Janakpur was reported quiet, in the neighbouring district, Mahottari, police fired on a crowd resulting in one death and one person injured. Indeed, there were reports of disturbances across the *terai* – with what one source describes as 'burning, thrashing, destruction of bridges, barricading of roads' (Sah 2017: 285). There can be no doubt that peasants from the region were involved, but this was more than a classic peasant revolt.

The Communist Party Divided

As we have already seen, following the demise of the Jhapa uprising, M. B. Singh, together with other Maoists including

Nirmal Lama, had formed the Central Nucleus of the Communist Party which, following a Fourth Party Congress or Convention in September 1974, became known as the CPN (Fourth Congress or Convention). Its strategy was to launch a people's movement of peasants and workers in the rural areas that could at the right moment be converted into an armed revolt.

The death of Mao Tse Tung and the overthrow of the 'Gang of Four' in China led to intense ideological struggle within the communist movement, particularly among the Maoists. The Ma-Le had not entirely rejected armed struggle and later in 1979, a proposal for training guerrillas, 'proletarianising' party cadres, creating separate base areas, taking action against local cheats, and initiating an 'agrarian uprising' was adopted. The Ma-Le also launched a student movement in 1979. In the CPN Fourth Congress, Nirmal Lama recognized the new Chinese leadership, but M. B. Singh denounced 'Chinese revisionism', labelled the Chinese leadership under Deng Hsiao Ping as 'counter-revolutionaries', and pledged allegiance to orthodox Maoism and the Cultural Revolution.

The Warrior Revolutionary & 'Che' Guevara

Ram Raja Prasad Singh, a political activist whom C. K. Lal has described as "the warrior revolutionary" (Lal 2013) was born in 1936 in Saptari district in the eastern *terai*. Ram Raja recalls one particular incident from his childhood: during a rally organized by the Quit India Movement just across the border from his home, he witnessed a shooting. As the protester died, some of the other dissidents applied his blood to their foreheads and began to shout, 'He has attained martyrdom; he is a martyr'. The incident remained vivid in Singh's memory many years later: 'I realized how sacrosanct was the blood of a revolutionary'.

His father sent him to Banaras Hindu University (BHU), where he spent four years studying English literature and Liberal Arts; but after joining a general strike he got himself expelled. He tried other schools but eventually ended up at the University of Delhi, where he mixed with many different kinds of radicals and effectively began his revolutionary career. In his memoir, Ram Raja recalls his friendship with a South American girl named Clara, who, in 1961 arranged for him and some of his friends to meet Ernesto 'Che' Guevara on an island off the Burmese coast. C. K. Lal comments that, 'nearly half a century after that meeting, Singh still became excited at the mere memory of Che's charisma' (Lal 2013: 84). Lal tells us that 'Singh translated some of Che's essays into Nepali, although none of them can now be traced'.

After finishing his studies in Delhi, Ram Raja read law at Bihar University and then returned to Nepal in 1964. Three years later, he contested one of the four seats reserved for national graduates in the assembly elections. He argued that 'political transformation in Nepal had to undergo the process of representation, persuasion, agitation, and revolution'. 'Revolutionaries', he declared, should be prepared for 'the annihilation of the old order'. Given such an apocalyptic vision, he was unsurprisingly arrested, barred from the election, and charged with sedition. He secured his release through his familial connections to the Indian establishment and by persuading the court that he had only discussed the theoretical stages of revolution and was therefore not guilty.

By the 1970s, Ram Raja and his party, the Nepali Congress Party (NCP), had begun to disagree about the best strategy for building democracy in Nepal. The Party leadership had lost faith in armed struggle and had handed over their weapons to insurrectionists in East Pakistan. In contrast, Ram Raja, along with many others in the NCP and the Nepali communist movement, thought that reform from within was impossible. Some of these communists began to take up arms (as we have seen), but Ram Raja decided to try a different approach. Once again he ran as a graduate constituency candidate for the national assembly but promoting a platform that called for an end to the undemocratic *panchayat* system, and warning that if this did not come about, armed struggle might be the only path.

On 22 October 1971, the *Naya Sandeh* weekly reported on a speech Ram Raja made in Biratnagar, writing that the candidate 'went beyond the limits' and told the audience, 'if the *panchayat* system is not abolished peacefully . . . the leaves of the trees will turn into bombs, grains of paddy will become bullets'. He won his seat, marking a significant defeat for the regime, but the state prevented him from taking an oath of office and arrested him. After a special tribunal convicted him, King Mahendra invited him to the palace, a method the monarchy used to woo dissenters, granted him a royal pardon and allowed him to take his place in the assembly.

In 1975, he again toured the country, this time in his official capacity as a NCP activist and an assembly member. His rousing speeches decried the regime's undemocratic control over the nation. Once again, he was expelled from the national assembly and arrested. Indeed, he spent much of his time over the next few years in and out of jail. In 1976, he established the Nepal Democratic Front as a left-wing political movement; the party changed its name to the Multi-Party Democratic Front when King Birendra called a referendum to decide the future of the *panchayat* system in 1980.

To prepare for the vote, other prominent NCP activists were released from jail. The whole spectrum of communist parties — some of which, like the CPN (Fourth Convention) or CPN (Masal) under M. B. Singh, refused to endorse the referendum but were prepared to participate in it. Ram Raja himself began to call not only for multi-party democracy but also for a constituent assembly; in the meanwhile he began to prepare for an armed struggle. He began recruiting fighters from the NCP's left wing, while seeking out weapons and support further afield. He tried to establish training camps in his old stomping ground of Bihar and reached out to the Tamil freedom fighters and Tiger Siddiqui, the nephew of the assassinated Bangladeshi Prime Minister Mujibur Rahman.

When this proved unsuccessful, he went to Chambal, a remote forested region of Uttar Pradesh, and bought guns from the bandits who operated there. One of them recommended that he use explosives rather than guns, and he took this advice. He returned to Nepal and recruited some ex-servicemen from the Nepal army to train his young guerrillas. C. K. Lal remarks that 'not much is known about what Singh and his band of guerrillas did between 1980 and 1985 — he claims they were being trained in handling fire-arms and explosives in different locations around northern India'. Whatever they were doing, they felt sufficiently prepared to act in the summer of 1985. When they did, they intervened not in the rural areas but in the towns, not with guns but with bombs.

10

Rural Unrest in the 1980s

Divisions on the Left

The Maoist faction led by Nirma Lal broke with M. B. Singh's faction in 1983-84, but continued to operate – albeit now as a separate party – under the name of the CPN (Fourth Congress). Singh and others formed the CPN (Masal). In March 1984, the CPN (Masal) joined the Revolutionary Internationalist Movement (RIM) as a founder member. A year later, the CPN (Masal) divided into two groups, confusing called CPN (Masal) and CPN (Mashal) – the former led by M. B. Singh and Babu Ram Bhattarai, and the latter by Mohan Baidya (later known as 'Kiran'). It was in the CPN (Mashal) that Pushpa Kamal Dahal (later known as 'Prachanda') became a leading figure and general secretary in 1989. In 1990, all of these groups, except for the CPN (Masal) under M. B. Singh, would split finally from the CPN (Fourth Congress) and united under the leadership of 'Prachanda' as the CPN (Unity Centre).

In May 1985, the Nepali Congress Party - which through the 1970s had been involved in an armed struggle against the Panchayat System that involved mainly sporadic bombings in urban areas, particularly in the eastern *terai,* but also an armed insurgency (the previously mentioned 'the Timburbote Incident') - launched a campaign of civil disobedience (*satyagraha*), starting with a general strike and a 'fill the jails' campaign. The movement appeared to be gaining ground when a series of bombings took place in June 1986, initiated by a group called the Nepal Janabadi Morcha (the People's Front), led by Ram Raja Prasad Singh, which aimed to overthrow the Panchayat System, topple the monarchy, install a democratic republic and abolish private property.

That May, the NCP had called for a civil disobedience action (*satyagraha*), which won support from other left-wing activists, including most of the communist parties. The media described the event as a sign of a gathering storm. Then, on June 20, 1985, a series of coordinated blasts in the capital and in other cities rocked Nepal. At least eight people died, including a member of parliament. In Kathmandu, explosions went off near the royal palace, at the Hotel de l'Annapurna, at the prime minister's office, and near the national assembly, where a politician was killed. A staff member at the Annapurna Hotel also lost her life. In Pokhara, the person responsible for the bomb was killed, and another woman died in Birgunj. Bombs also went off at the Bhairahawa airport, Nepalganj and Mahendranagar in the west, and Janakpur, Biratnagar, and Jhapa in the east.

Ram Raja Singh and his guerrillas admitted responsibility but defended their actions. They explained that they had planned the bombing at the national assembly for a holiday, believing no one would be there. Unfortunately, the rain drove some people to take shelter, turning them into unintended victims. Likewise, the guerillas had left the explosive device on the Annapurna Hotel's lawn, but someone had inadvertently deposited it in the lobby. After the explosions, hundreds were arrested and the Destructive Crimes (Special Control and Punishment Act) was rushed through Parliament. Singh was charged and found guilty in absentia. He, his brother Laxman, Bisheshwar Mandal, and Prem Bahadur Vishwakarma were given the death penalty;

others received life sentences, and many had their property confiscated. These named leaders went underground, but five others disappeared while in custody.

After the first spectacular attacks, Singh's operations in Nepal could not continue. He was subsequently arrested in India, but was later released him secretly and allowed to live quietly in Patna. His guerrilla war ended, almost without trace. After G. P. Koirala became the first elected prime minister of the new multi-party democratic order in 1990, however, the state withdrew all charges against him. He even stood as an NCP candidate in the mid-term elections of 1994, but he lost badly and retired finally to live the rest of his days in India. It is not clear what happened to the others involved in his short-lived guerrilla war.

Rural Unrest in the Western *terai*

Encouraged by the success in 1967 of the 148 *sukumbasi* families led by Chilla Tharu in obtaining land and rights to settle and farm, even if they were subsequently driven off, in 1980, Janglee Tharu led 1,300 Tharu *sukumbasi* families to settle in Machar in Dhodari VDC, where they lived for two years, providing labour for the villages of Sonshree and Tarataal. Many of those were Deshaura Tharu and Ek Saro Kamaiyas. One of the problems faced by the Kanara *sukumbasi* was that the small size of their plots meant that they had to supplement agriculture and livestock production with wage labour. So they had to find work in nearby VDCs or in towns, like Gulariya and Lali Bazaar. They also were able to take advantage of work on the Kothariyaghat road project, which offered ample opportunities for labourers.

In 1982, they moved to Sirkaina as Machar was some five hours distance walking from Sonshree and Tarataal where they were employed. They were evicted from Sirkaina, however, by government officials and their homes were destroyed, using elephants and bulldozers. They were then forcibly taken to Jogi village in Kairepur VDC and to Gulariya. That day there were heavy rains and 35 children died in the move. Most of them eventually were given one third of a hectare of land, but some did not receive land.

In 1985, Dilli Chaudhary and some friends started a youth club in Dumri Gaun in Dang District, organized around literacy classes and other activities. The club was supported for some years by an NGO called No Frills, which in turn was working with the Vegetable, Fruit and Cash Crops Project (VFCCP) funded by USAID. The club was encouraged to reformulate itself as a 4-H club, along the lines developed in the 1960s in the USA as part of a community development movement; and in its new guise the group was named the Dumri Gaun Misrit Caar Patte Club, or Dumri Gaun Youth Club. Gradually, the club began to become more politicized and to take on other activities, including confronting landlords in disputes.

The club changed its name again to Sramik Mukti Sangata (Labourers' Liberation Organization) and among other activities, began to organize a strike by agricultural labourers. It lost the support of the USAID funded VFC CP, and suffered from the loss of funding. But, in 1988, Dilli Chaudhary was able, with the help of No Frills, to attend a meeting of the Asian Adhivasi Committee in Thailand. Through the contacts established there, he subsequently visited India and learned more about the tribal rights movements there (Cox, cited in Fujikura 2011: 64). After 1990, the group was able to register as an NGO under the name of BASE – Backward Society Education - and was able to attract funding from DANIDA and other agencies.

In the meanwhile, *sukumbasis* in Nawalparasi continued to resist the indiscriminate eviction of large numbers of households in Nawalpur during the early 1980s. A large demonstration was organized, for example, and held in Kawasoti Bazaar in Nawalparasi on 14 March 1983. Police fired on the demonstration and several people, including the president of the district panchayat (who supported the local land rights movement) were arrested and detained in Bhairahawa jail (Ghimire 1992: 145-146).

Karki reports that 'from the early 1980s until 1990, a series of similar demonstrations took place throughout the *terai* belt of Nepal, attempting to establish land rights, mainly concentrated ... in Chitwan, Nawalparasi, Banke, Bardiya, Kailali and Kanchanpur Districts' (2002: 13). We do not have details of all of these local peasant land rights movements in the *terai,* but Conway and Shrestha (1981: 226) considered them political significant, while Kaplan and Shrestha referred to the '*sukumbasi* movement in Nepal' as 'the fire from below' (1982: 75). Ghimire makes it clear that government concerns about the 'problems for law and order' posed by 'large and growing illegal settlement' dated back to the mid-1970s (Ghimire 1992: 5) and traces the evolution of the evolution of 'popular discontent' and of 'official responses' to local demands for land from as far back as the 1960s (Ghimire 1992: 130-146).

11

Rural Unrest in the 1990s

The People's Movement (Jana Andolan)

During the late 1980s, all of the left political groups were involved in the mobilization of various sections of Nepali society in opposition to the Panchayat System and the status quo, including peasants and agricultural workers. Finally, in 1989, the Ma-Le leadership considered the time ripe to launch another major political thrust. They convened a Fourth Convention and some 90 delegates met under tight security in August in the forest in Udaypur District, near Siraha. They decided to call on all of the 11 communist party factions and groupings, and the Nepali Congress Party, to form an alliance to bring an end to the Panchayat System.

In early 1990, an alliance of seven communist parties had been created as a United Left Front to constitute, together with the Nepali Congress Party, a broader Movement for the Restoration of Multi-Party Democracy. This included, among others, the Workers and Peasants Party of Comrade Rohit. Already, however, many communists were skeptical of the possibilities of radical transformation provided by the new dispensation and started building a grass-roots underground revolutionary movement while at the same time forming a United Front to fight elections and present a more moderate face. During February and March

1990, support for the 'democracy movement' had grown to the point where it could longer be ignored. There were mass demonstrations in most of the major cities and all across the country. Peasants and agricultural workers were also involved, but this was a good deal more than a peasant movement – it was a mass People's Movement (Jana Andolan) – and it brought about dramatic and far-reaching, even if not revolutionary, changes.

In April 1990, the Panchayat System effectively came to an end. It seemed, for a time, that a new multi-party democracy was being born, albeit with a constitutional monarchy still in place, and that a progressive transformation of the political economy of Nepal was imminent. In the events that followed, however, the grass roots movement that had been effectively mobilized by the communists was increasingly marginalized and its demands – which included the formation of a Constituent Assembly to draft a new Constitution – were ignored.

The Maoist Response

The two Masal/Mashal groups and the Revolutionary Workers' Party united to form the Samyukta Rastriya Jana Andolan (The United National People's Movement – UNPM) and joined the street protests of April 1990 once the People's Movement had gained momentum but maintained an organizational distance from it. The CPN (Mashal) did not, for example, as a party join the other communists and the NCP in the Movement for the Restoration of Democracy, although many of its members were active in the demonstrations that had begun in February 1990.

Even the United Left Front soon found itself in a distinct minority in the interim government that was formed in May 1990, and its demands for a Constituent Assembly, originally promised in 1951, went unheeded. The UNPM, which also called for a Constituent Assembly to draft a new national Constitution was equally sidelined. Instead, a drafting committee framed a new Constitution, based on a Westminster-type parliamentary, while the Palace produced its own version. Faced with mass demonstrations organized by all the left forces, the king was obliged to compromise and in negotiation with the Nepali Congress Party formulated the final version of the new Constitution, in November 1990 and established the framework for elections to be held the following May.

The UNPM rejected this new Constitution and initially decided to boycott the elections. The same month, however, the Communist Party of Nepal (Unity Centre – Ekata Kendra) was established, with Pushpa Kamal Dahal ('Prachanda') as General Secretary. The Unity Centre, like the UNPM, rejected the November 1990 Constitution and continued to call for a Constituent Assembly, a new democratic Constitution and eventually the formation of a People's Republic. Shortly afterwards, in January 1991, one of the young Mashal leaders, Baburam Bhattarai, organized an alliance of leftist groups under the name of the United People's Front – Samyukta Jan Morcha (SJM) or United People's Front of Nepal (UPFN).

The Unity Centre and UPFN brought together several Maoist parties: the CPN (Mashal) under Prachanda, the CPN (Fourth Congress) under Nirmal Lama, the Proletariat Workers' Organization under Ruplal Bishwakarma, the CPN (Marxist) under Sahana Pradhan, the CPN (Marxist-Leninist-Maoist – MLM) under Krishna Das, the Nepal Workers and Peasants Party under Narayan Man Bikukchhe (Rohit), and a splinter group of the CPN (Masal), led by Dr Babu Ram Bhattarai – which had broken away from the main CPN (Masal) still led by Mohan Bikram Singh.

In the meanwhile, the two major communist parties – the CPN (Marxist), the remnants of Pushpa Lal's original party, and the CPN (Marxist-Leninist or ML), founded by the leaders of the Jhapa Movement and the largest left organization at this time – joined together with some other smaller groupings on the left, to form the Nepal Communist Party (United Marxist-Leninist – UML) in early 1991. The CPN (UML) participated in the first general election in May 1991 and became not only the mainstream communist party but, together with the Nepali Congress Party, one of the two major parties in Nepal. The UML won 69 seats with just over 2 million votes, while the Nepali Congress Party gained 110 seats with a vote of 2.75 million.

The CPN (Unity Centre) fought the election as the Samyukta Jan Morch (SJM) or United People's Front of Nepal (UPFN) with Babu Ram Bhattarai as the coordinator, and won nine seats with just over 350,000 votes ad gained the status of a national party with more than 3 per cent of the total vote. Its seats were won in Siraha and Ramechhap in the east, in Lalitpur in the Kathmandu Valley and in Kavrepalanchowk in the hills to the north of Kathmandu, in Chitwan in the central terai, in Rolpa (with two MPs) in the mid-western hills, and in Humla in the remote northwest. This made it the third largest party in parliament. Even before the elections, however, the Rohit group had withdrawn from the UPFN and the MLM withdrew shortly afterwards; others also gradually withdrew over the next year or so.

The CPN (Unity Centre) held its first congress in December 1991 and decided to adopt Marxism-Leninism-Maoism as the ideological 'direction' of the Party and the path of protracted People's War along the line of the classic Chinese model, rather than the mass uprising proposed by Nirmal Lama, as the appropriate revolutionary strategy for Nepal. Not only did it reject 'the parliamentary road', therefore, but also the urban-centred mass uprising in favour of an armed struggle rooted in the peasantry. The Unity Centre remained 'semi-underground' but the UPFN was to remain active and 'in the open'. The UPFN fared badly in the 1992 elections, but in April-May 1992 a UPFN-led general strike plunged the country into nation-wide violence. The local CPN (Unity Centre) party cadres, particularly in Rolpa and Rukum were now increasingly subject to harassment, arrests and ill-treatment by the authorities and the police as well as by Nepali Congress Party activists (see Karki & Seddon 2003: 20).

There followed a period of intense debate regarding strategy, tactics, timing and other aspects of the programme of 'armed struggle'. Several members of the Nirma Lal group were expelled from the UPFN and the CPN (Unity Centre) split into two. Increasingly after 1993-94, once they had decided not to participate in parliamentary politics, the political cadres of the UPFN and other leftist parties in Rolpa and Rukum, where they were particularly strong, were harassed by district government representatives and local authorities as well as by activists from the Nepali Congress Party. The Human Rights Yearbook for 1993 reports continuing repression and brutality directed against the UPFN.

In 1994-95, some 500 individual criminal charges were filed by the local authorities against UPFN party workers (Karki 2001: 169) and many of the accused – most of whom were grass-roots party activists – were obliged to flee their home and even their home districts as they could fund no-one prepared to defend them against these charges. In 1995, the Human Rights Yearbook reported that 'the government initiated… suppressive operations to a degree of state terror'. It stated that nearly 6,000 locals had left their villages as a result of police operations under the code name R for Romeo adding that under the leadership of ruling Nepali Congress Party workers, police searched, arrested and tortured people in numerous villages throughout the two districts of Rolpa and Rukum.

12

Tharu Movements

During the 1990s, BASE became more than an NGO, it became the catalyst for a movement for the emancipation of bonded labourers *(kamaiyas)* across the western *terai* and built a base of some 130,000 members (according to Fujikura 2011: 60, 62). As to how BASE was able to make the transition to a mass movement is debatable. Fujikura argues that BASE accumulated its resources and its legitimacy 'through operating in the field of development'. He summarises the 'story' of BASE as follows: 'a local youth group, by assuming a role in the US funded rural development project, became a participant in a transnational circuit and ideas and practices of development. And, through this participation, the group became a participant in a transnational circuit of ideas and activism of tribal rights and freedom struggles' (2011: 64).

He also suggests that it was able to remain independent of political parties and yet exert pressure on them. He then extends this argument to a more general one: 'my contention is that development discourses have been transforming the socio-political terrain in Nepal for the past five decades, and thus inquiry into the conditions of politics in the present requires one to engage with the effects of those development discourses' (2011: 62).

My own 'reading' of the 'story' however is very different. It is that the youth group became more radical and effectively fell out with the main USAID funded project (VFCCP) and experienced problems in funding. The support of the NGO No Frills, however, helped Dill Chaudhary make contact with activists in other countries and so inspire him to further develop the activities of BASE, and to establish the Kamaiya Mukti Parichalan Samiti, described by BASE as 'a popular movement led by young Tharus, with such objectives as empowerment of the oppressed and freedom for the *kamaiyas*'.

Fujikura himself also seems to question his own interpretation when he states that '... after 1990, with the donor money flowing in, not only for its primary, but extremely popular, activity of non-formal education classes, but also for other conventional programs such as health and women's savings groups, BASE had become more 'project oriented'. However, recently, BASE has again taken the form of a movement, succeeding in *kamaiya* emancipation, and now intends to continue focusing on movements, rather than projects' (2011: 61, referring to developments in 2000 and thereafter). This takes us into a very interesting area of debate regarding the relationship between development and political discourses and narratives, for many (eg Ferguson) have argued powerfully that the development discourse tends to de-politicize, whereas Fujikura seems to be saying that it can be – and has been generally – transformative in Nepal. Also, it raises all of the questions raised by Stacy Pigg and others regarding the 'unintended consequences' of development theory and practice, which we do not intend to pursue here.

BASE was, however, not the only movement involving Tharus in the western *terai* that developed during the 1990s. In April 1991, after more than a decade of working to organize such a thing, a 12 member committee was formed by the Tharu *sukumbasis* of Bardiya district – the Sarvahara Bhumihinm Sukumvasi Samittee, commonly known as the Kanara Mul

Samitee - under the chairmanship of Jagga Prashad Pandey, a non-Tharu, whose general secretary was Kashi Ram Tharu. Shortly afterward, sukumbasi from the different parts of Bardiya District moved to settle in the Kanara area. It seems that few actual *kamaiayas* participated in this movement; those who did so were mainly squatters originally from outside the *terai.*

Within a short time, Jagga Prashad Pandey was ousted from the committee and Resham Bahara Chaudhari became chair. Jagga Prashad then led a small section of the *sukumbasi* and started to settle them, also in the Kanara. He was accused of splitting the settler movement. In 1992, the government evicted the settlers forcibly but they then organized a move to the district headquarters and a sit-in and a relay hunger strike. According to some sources Runche Tharu died during this defiant action. Badhu Chaudhary, the general secretary of the Kanara Mul Samittee, described the condition of the Kanara squatters after government demolished their homes, recalling it as 'one of the worst tragedies of their lives by many Kanaras of that time' (cited in Dhakal 2013: 140).

Most of the men went to Gulariya, the district headquarters to protest against the brutal treatment by the government and to demand the restoration of their settlements. But the rest were without protection and homeless; not satisfied by the destruction of their homes, the police and forest guards would urinate in the water sources and on their walls. Eventually, some felt obliged to move to a nearby area, called Baniyabhar, an hour's walk to the northwest from Kanara. Here some 10 to 12 families settled under some trees. After two days, the weather turned bad, destroying their flimsy huts and killing seven people and injuring many more. One of the female activists of the Kanara Andolan, Kaushala Tharu, recalled that 'there was a mother, holding her six-month old baby. The baby was crying, but the mother was already dead. The rest of the survivors were in an extremely poor condition, and many of them were injured. Had there been any government sympathy, we would never have suffered such a miserable time; (we would have been) on our own land' (cited by Dhakal 2013: 140).

Dilendra Prasad Badu, the Assistant Minister for Housing and Physical Planning came to 'settle' the *sukumbasi* problem and later another minister and a DIG of police visited the area, but no solution could be agreed. In 1993, the government established a Sukumbasi Samasya Samadhan Aayoga (Squatters' Problems Resolution Commission) and a central member, Tek Bahadur Chokhyal, was assigned to take care of the issue. An all-party meeting concluded that the *sukumbasi* families of the Kanara would be brought together on the banks of the Babai River for two months and then re-settled elsewhere, but they would be allowed to harvest their crops in the Kanara area. This ended the sit-in protests.

They went back for the harvest, but found cattle grazing on their crops. The forest guards were responsible for this. The *sukumbasis* protested and requested that the guards desist; but they were beaten up and twelve of them several injured. This was in mid-December 1993. This was when sixty-year old Runche Tharu was killed, according to some accounts. He died of his injuries a few days later and became 'the first martyr of the Kanara Andolan' (Dhakal 2013: 142).

The Commission then began allocating land to some of the *sukumbasis*. This led to a change in the strategy of the Kanara Mul Samittee, since their principal demand – for land – was now apparently being fulfilled. In 1994, Kashi Ram Tharu, the general secretary of the Kanara Mul Samittee was elected as an MP. But the support of the *sukumbasis* remained a vital part of his electoral success. Eventually, during 1994 and 1995, the government re-settled all 4,939 Kanara squatter families in different parts of Bardiya District, in 42 different villages, involving a total population of 18,356 people. This spatial relocation and separation made the old forms of organization more difficult.

At this point, in 1995, SPACE, in partnership with SAPLANEER carried out a pilot study to assess the feasibility of intervention. This was followed up in 1996 by a detailed survey of six different settlements in three VDCs. All of these re-settled families had previously lived in the Kanara (in 1991-93). This survey also recorded aspects of the Kanara Andolan. In 1996, the Kamaiya Mukti Manch (Kamaiya Liberation Front) was set up by a gathering of some 300 *kamaiyas* in Nepalgunj under the chairmanship of Kashi Ram Tharu, tharu MP elected by eh squatters to represent them and former member of the Kanara Mul Samittee. This change actually weakened the Kanara Andolan in some respects; on the other hand, it inspired many Kanara Andolan activists to stand for local elections in 1997. Some were successful and became elected representatives for their communities in elections that were held at all levels locally from VDC to District.

Other Peasant Movements

In 1995, a movement erupted in Rasuwa which was referred to as the 'no grain payment' movement. *Birta* owners had been officially abolished but tenants were still obliged to pay grain to their former landlords. The tenants worked together to stop grain payments even on *guthi* land which was often land converted from *birta* earlier.

In 1996, a new land rights movement, initiated by the National Land Rights Forum (NLRF) and the Community Self-Reliance Centre (CSRC) in Sindhupalchowk, was launched when 42 cases were filed at the District Land Reform Office. This was, as Jagat

Basnet commented in 2008, 'the beginning of the present land rights movement which is getting more and more recognition at the national level' (Basnet 2008: 28).

In 1997, the *bagdari* and the *pitmari* land rights movements were launched in Bardiya and Banke Districts respectively by land hungry peasants. The government tried its best to suppress these movements. In 1998, land belonging to a land resettlement company was seized by the landless people of Banke.

13

Towards the People's War

The Communist Party of Nepal (Maoist) – CPN(M)

Even as Operation Romeo took place, the Maoists initiated a campaign (the Sija Campaign) to propagate Maoist ideology among the local population, whose aim was explicitly 'to arouse the masses and heighten political consciousness' (Karki & Seddon 2003: 20). The repression had the effect of stiffening the resolve of the Maoists and their supporters; and in March 1995, at the third plenum of the central committee, the Unity Centre (Maoist) changed its name to the Communist Party of Nepal (Maoist) and formally adopted 'the strategy and tactics of armed struggle in Nepal'. The struggle was to take place essentially in the countryside and to involve workers and peasants for the most part, although the potential for urban unrest was not ignored.

The statement issued declared that 'the conscious peasant class struggle developed in the western hill districts, particularly in Rolpa and Rukum, represents the high level of anti-feudal and anti-imperialist revolutionary struggle. That struggle has given birth to some new tendencies in the Nepal communist movement which have inspired us to be more serious about the business of armed struggle' (cited in Karki & Seddon 2003: 18). This makes it very clear that the leadership of the CPN (M) regarded the struggle as essentially a 'peasant class struggle' at this point. In this sense, it followed the broad Maoist tradition.

By now the CPN (Maoist) had also joined the Revolutionary Internationalist Movement (RIM) which provided it with support and encouragement. The RIM was an international Communist organization founded in France in March 1984 by 17 Maoist organizations around the world. It sought to 'struggle for the formation of a Communist International of a new type, based on Marxism–Leninism–Maoism'. The CPN (Masal) had previously been a founder member, but later (in October 1996) left the RIM over differences of 'political line' (discussed in detail by Yogendra Dhakal writing as Ajay Sharma (nd: 292). The RIM also supported the struggles led by the Communist Party of the Philippines and by the Communist Party of India (Maoist).

In late January/early February 1996, the SJM/UPFN issued a statement, condemning the 'barbaric oppression of the people of Rolpa and Rukum by the Nepali Congress government' and demanding the dismissal of the Chief District Officer of Rolpa, the cancellation of all criminal charges/cases and the release of all those detained and implicated. It demanded an end to 'administrative repression and state terrorism' and called for an independent investigation. The same month, it submitted a 40-point list of demands on behalf of the CPN (Maoist) to the Nepali Congress Party government of Sher Bahadur Deuba – a list that Thapa remarks were not much different from the points outlined in the 1991 election manifesto of the SJM/UPFN (Thapa 2002: 82).

The memorandum strongly criticized the perpetuation of the Hindu kingdom and called for a republican Constitution drawn up by a Constitutent Assembly elected by universal suffrage. It also expressed a nationalist hostility towards 'Western imperialism' (including international 'development aid') and 'Indian expansionism', demanding for example that all treaties with India that ensured Nepal's dependency should be rescinded.

In the absence of a response from the government, on 13 February 1996, the CPN (Maoist) launched the People's War in Nepal, issuing a leaflet that called on 'the people of Nepal' to 'march along the path of the People's War to smash the reactionary state and establish a New Democratic State'.

The stated objectives were: 'to overthrow the bureaucratic-capitalist class and state system, to uproot semi-feudalism and to drive out imperialism, in order to establish a new democratic republic with a view to building a new socialist society'. This, if anything, represented what Whelpton terms 'a crusade', although this is surely the wrong label for an insurgency that was inspired by Maoist principles and aimed to overthrow the regime through the armed struggle of a People's War? In so far as the support for this struggle, in the form of cadres and guerrilla fighters, was provided largely by the workers and peasants of Nepal, this was surely one of what Wolf referred to as the 'peasant wars of the 20th century' (Wolf 1971). We intend to explore the extraordinary political and military phenomenon of the People's War in Nepal, in another work.

Conclusion

We have tried, in this small book, to provide an overview of the long two hundred year history of rural unrest in Nepal, from the period of 'unification' in the 1790s to the launching of the People's War in 1996. It is clearly a 'work in progress', as there are numerous instances of rural unrest where we have only the barest details. We hope that more of this history of rural unrest will be 'uncovered' in the coming years, and also hope that this work may stimulate others to undertake the necessary archival and fieldwork that will be required.

We have also tried to show that, even if it may often be useful to distinguish different forms of rural unrest, the phenomenon is itself complex and multi-faceted, and it is not always easy to distinguish a grass-roots peasant revolt or movement from something orchestrated from above, or a rural rebellion from the arena of elite politics. It is also often the case that it is usually not a matter of 'either...or', but of both. Furthermore, in so far as many peasants in Nepal identify themselves as members of one ethnic group or another, or as members of one caste or another, it is often easy to characterize peasant movements as ethnic movements, or as movements driven by caste relationships. In such cases, it is again usually not a matter of 'either... or' but of multiple causation and complex interactions of class, caste and ethnicity.

Finally, we are all too aware that in many cases, the individuals involved cannot be identified, and there is therefore a tendency to generalise – ie *sukumbasi,* tenants, labourers, peasants – without distinguishing men and women, old and young, and precise class position, which as Wolf argued in his *Peasant Wars of the Twentieth Century,* is often crucial. Where we have been able to identify individuals, and draw attention to the fact that women were almost always involved in some capacity in the struggle for rights to land, to livelihoods and to human dignity, we have done so.

This book is dedicated to all those who struggled for their rights over two centuries of change in Nepal, to all those who continue to do so, and to all those who work with them to achieve a more secure and better life.

References & Bibliography

Adhikari, Jagannath. (2008). *Land Reform in Nepal: Problems and Prospects.* Kathmandu: ActionAid Nepal.

Adhikari, S. (1998). *Jumla Rajyako Itihas.* Kirtipur: Tribhuvan University.

Aziz, Barbara Nimri. (2001). *Heir to a Silent Song: Two Rebel Women of Nepal.* Kathmandu: Centre for Nepal and Asian Studies (CNAS), Tribhuvan University.

Aziz, Barbara Nimri. (1993). *Shakti Yogmaya: A Tradition of Dissent in Nepal.* Kathmandu: Centre for Nepal and Asian Studies, Tribhuvan University.

Bailey, Anne. (1974). *On the Specificity of the Asiatic Mode of Production.* M. Phil. thesis, University of London.

Baral, Thakur. (2058 vs). *Atitka Janasanghharsha (Peoples' Movements of the Past).* Dhankuta: Byanjana, Kshitiz and Sindhu Baral.

Basnet, Jagat. et al. (2010). *Asserting Freedom from Central Control,* Nepal Country Paper, Land Watch Asia, Securing the Right to Land. Kathmandu: Action Aid International, International Land Coalition & MISEREOR.

Basnet, Jagat. (2008). 'Overview of Land Rights Movements in Nepal'. In (eds) Bishnu Upreti et al. *Land Politics and Conflict in Nepal.*

Bhattarai, Gopal, B. (2062 vs). *Dhankuta Chintang ko Itihas (History of Dankhuta Chintang).* Dhankuta: Hima Devi Basnet Bhattarai.

Bhushal, S.K. (2008). *Kapilvastu ma Bhumi Samasya ek Parichya (An Introduction to Land Problems in Kapilvastu).* Kapilvastu: Kapilvastu Sansthagat Bikas Samiti.

Bijukche, N. M. (2059 vs). *Saya Barsha Pachiko Bhakatpur (Bhaktapur after a hundred years).* Bhaktapur: Kendriay Prakshan Samiti, Nepal Majdur Kishan Party.

Bishop, Barry. (1990). *Karnali Under Stress: livelihood strategies and seasonal rhythms in a changing Nepal Himalaya.* Chicago: University of Chicago Press.

Blaikie, Piers., Cameron, John., & Seddon David (1980, 2001) *Nepal in Crisis: growth and stagnation at the periphery.* Delhi: Oxford University Press.

Blaikie, Piers., John Cameron., & Seddon, David. (1979). *The Struggle for Basic Needs in Nepal.* Warminster: Aris & Phillips.

Budhathoki, Padma Bahadur. (2048 vs.). *Nepalma Kishan Andolan (The Peasant Movement in Nepal)*, Bhaktapur.

Cailmail, Benoit. (2013). The CPN (Masal) Bastion: a history of communist militancy in Pyuthan District and its influence on the People's War. In (ed) Marie Lecomte-Tilouine, *Revolution in Nepal: an anthropological and historical approach to the People's War.* Delhi: Oxford University Press.

Cailmail, Benoit. (2008-09). A History of Nepalese Maoism since its Foundation by Mohan Bikram Singh. *European Bulletin of Himalayan Research*, nos. 33-34, Autumn 2008-Spring 2009, pp. 11-38.

Caplan, Lionel. (1970). *Land and Social Change in East Nepal: a study of Hindu-tribal relations*, London: Routledge & Kegan Paul.

CERM. (1971). *Sur le Féodalisme*, Centre d'Etudes et de Recherches Marxistes. Paris: Editions Sociales.

CERM. (1970). *Sur les societiés précapitalistes*, Centre d'Etudes et de Recherches Marxistes. Paris: Editions Sociales.

CERM. (1969). Sur le 'Mode de Production Asiatique'. Centre d'Etudes et de Recherches Marxistes. Paris: Editions Sociales).

Conway, D., & Shrestha N. R. (1981). *Causes and Consequences of Rural to Rural Migration in Nepal.* Indiana: Indiana University Press.

Cox, Thomas. (1990). 'Land rights and ethnic conflicts in Nepal' *Economic & Political Vernacular Nepali Weekly*, 16 June 1990, pp. 1318-1320.

Communist Party of Nepal (CPN) (1949) *Nepal Communist Party Ko Pahilo Ghosana Patra (The First Manifesto of the Communist Party of Nepal)*, Kathmandu: CPN.

CPN-ML (2017 vs). *Barga Shangharsa (The Class Struggle).* Kathmandu: CPN-ML.

CSRC. (2006). *Haliya: Bhumi Adhikar Bare Padhne Samagri* (Haliya: Reading Material on Land Rights). Bhumi Adhikar (Land Rights), 3:2. Kathmandu: Community Self Reliance Centre.

Dhakal, Suresh. (2018). 'Peasant as Anthropological Category and Ethnographic Subject: a critical overview of peasantrty and peasant politics', in (eds) Laya Uprety, Suresh Dhakal & Jaga Basnet, *Peasant Studies in Nepal.* Kathmandu: Vajra Books.

Dhakal, Suresh. (2013). *Land and Agrarian Questions: Essays on Land Tenure, Agrarian Relations and Peasant Movements in Nepal.* Kathmandu: Community Self-Reliance Centre.

Dhakal, Suresh. (2013). 'Chintang Bidorha 1979, Locating a Peasant Movement in a Political Landscape'. In Suresh Dhakal. *Land and Agrarian Questions.* chapter 6.

Dhakal, Suresh. (2013). 'Kanara Andolan, A Case of Land Rights Movement'. In Suresh Khanal' *Land and Agrarian Questions.* chapter 7.

Dhakal, Suresh. (2011). *Land Tenure and Agrarian Reforms in Nepal.* Kathmandu: CSRC.

Dhakal, Suresh. (2007). 'Haruwa, the Unfree Agricultural Labourer: a case study from the eastern terai', *Contributions to Nepalese Studies,* vol.34, no.2., July 2007

Feldman, David., & Fournier, Alain. (1976). 'Social relations and agricultural production in Nepal's *terai*'. *The Journal of Peasant Studies,* vol.3, no.4, pp. 447-464.

Fitzpatrick, Ian Carlos. (2011). *Cardamom and Class: a Limbu village and its extensions in East Nepal.* Kathmandu: Vajra Publications.

Gallissot, René. (1975). 'Pre-Colonial Algeria'. *Economy & Society,* vol. 4, no. 4.

Gellner, David. N. (1997). 'Caste, Communalism and Communism' in (eds.) David N. Gellner, Joanna Pfaff-Czarnecka & John Whelpton, *Nationalism and Ethnicity in a Hindu Kingdom: the politics of culture in contemporary Nepal.* Harwood Academic Publishers

Gellner, Ernest. (1969). *Saints of the Atlas.* London: Weidenfeld & Nicolson.

Ghimire, Krishna. (1992) *Forest or Farm? The politics of poverty and land hunger in Nepal.* Delhi: Oxford University Press.

Hobsbawm, Eric. (1964). 'Introduction' to K. Marx, Pre-Capitalist Economic Formations. London: Lawrence & Wishart.

Hobsbawm, Eric. (1959). *Social Bandits and Primitive Rebels: studies in archaic forms of social movements in the 19th and 20th centuries.* Glencoe: The Free Press

INSEC. (1992). *Bonded Labour in Nepal under the Kamaya System.* Kathmandu: INSEC.

Kaplan, P., & Shrestha N. R. (1982) 'The Sukumbasi Movement in Nepal: the fire from below', *The Journal of Contemporary Asia,* vol. 12.

Karki, Arjun (2002) *The Politics of Poverty and Movements from Below,* Unpubl. PhD thesis, University of East Anglia.

Karki, Arjun. (2002). Movements from Below: land rights movements in Nepal. *Inter-Asia Cultural Studies*, vol.3, no 2, August.

Karki, Arjun., & Seddon, David. (2003). *The People's War in Nepal: left perspective*. Delhi: Adroit Publishers.

Kishan Sangharsha. (1977). *An Official Bulletin of the Nepal Mazdoor Kishan Party*, no.3, Bhaktapur.

Lacoste, Yves. (1974). 'General characteristics and fundamental structures of mediaeval North African society'. (translated by David Seddon). *Economy & Society*, vol.3, no.1.

Lal, C. K. (2013). Ram Raja Prasad Singh: the warrior revolutionary. In (ed) Marie Lecomte-Tilouine, *Revolution in Nepal: an anthropological and historical approach to the People's War*. Oxford: Oxford University Press.

Lecomte-Tilouine, Marie. (2013). *Revolution in Nepal: an anthropological and historical approach to the People's War*. Oxford: Oxford University Press.

Lecomte-Tilouine, Marie. (2003). 'The History of the Messianic and Rebel King Lakhan Thapa: Utopia and Ideology among the Magar'. In D. Gellner (ed) *Resistance and the State: Nepalese Experiences*. New Delhi: Social Science Press, pp. 244-78.

Lecomte-Tilouine, Marie. (2000). 'Utopia and Ideology among the Magars: Lakhan Thapa Versus Mao Dzedong?' *European Bulletin of Himalayan Research*, 19, 73-97.

Manandhar, Prabin., & Seddon, David. (2010). *In Hope and In Fear: living through the People's War in Nepal*. Delhi: Adroit Publishers.

Marx, Karl. *The Grundrisse – Notebook IV (Pre-Capitalist Economic Formations)*.

Mikesell, Stephen. (1999). *Class, State and Struggle in Nepal*. New Delhi: Manohar.

Murray, Robin. (1975). Class, state and the world economy: a case study of Ethiopia. Paper presented to the Conference on 'New Approaches to Trade', IDS, Sussex, September 1975.

Neupane, Dipesh. (2015). *The Synthesis between Social Protest and Nirguna Bhakti in Yogmaya's Sarvartha Yogbani*. Kathmandu: Tribhuvan University.

Neupane, Dipesh. (2012). *Spiritualism and Religious Fervor in Sarvartha Yogbani. Pursuits: A Journal of English Studies*, July 2012.

NRSU. (2011). 'The Role of Nepal Workers and Peasants' Party in the Communist Movement of Nepal'. The Workers' Bulletin, 1.1 (1): 1–6.

Pandey, Binu., & Rimal, Bishnu. (translation by Mukunda Kattel). (n.d.). *Women's Participation in Nepali Labour Movement.* Kathmandu: GEFONT.

Pokharel, C., & Basyal, R. (1999). *Rapti Paschim Ky Prajatantric Andolan (The Democratic Movement in West Rapti).* Bardiya: Subash Pokhrel.

Pradhan, Kumar. (1991, 2009). *The Gorkha Conquests: the process and consequences of the unification of Nepal with particular reference to eastern Nepal.* Calcutta: Oxford University Press & Kathmandu: Social Science Baha/Himal Books.

Raj, Yogesh. (2010). *History and Mindscapes: a Memory of the Peasants Movements of Nepal.* Kathmandu: Martin Chautari.

Rana, Prabhakar S. J. B., Rana, Pashupati S. J. B., & Rana, Gautam S. J. B. (2002). The Ranas of Nepal. Geneva: Edition Naef. Kister S.S. Editeur.

Rana, P.S. (2000). *A Chronicle of Rana Rule.* Kathmandu: R. Rana.

Rana, P.S. (1995). *Rana Intrigues.* Kathmandu: R. Rana.

Rana, P.S. (1978). *Rana Nepal - An Insider's View.* Kathmandu: R. Rana.

Rawal, Bhim. (2007). *The Communist Movement in Nepal*: Origin and Development. Kathmandu/Accham: Forum CPN (UML).

Regmi, Mahesh Chandra. (1999). *A Study of Nepali Economic History, 1768-1845.* New Delhi: Manjusri Publishing House; Delhi: Adroit Publishers.

Regmi, Mahesh Chandra. (1988.) *An Economic History of Nepal: 1846-1901.* Varanasi: Nath Publishing House.

Regmi, Mahesh Chandra. (1984). Bhote and Murmi Rebels. *Regmi Research Series*, 16: 129-30.

Regmi, Mahesh Chandra. (1977). *Land Ownership in Nepal.* Delhi: Adroit Publishers.

Regmi, Mahesh Chandra. (1963-68). *Land Tenure and Taxation in Nepal* (4 vols). Berkeley: Berkeley Institute of International Studies, University of California.

Sah, Ram Manohar. (2017). *The Middle Country: the traverse of Madhes through war, colonization and aid dependent racist state,* Delhi: Adroit Publishers.

Scott, James. (1985). *Weapons of the Weak: everyday forms of peasant resistance.* Yale University Press.

Seddon, David (2018). 'Resistance, Rebellion, Revolt and Revolution: a historical/ anthropological consideration of peasant movements and other forms of rural unrest in Nepal' in (eds) Laya Prasad Uprety, Sureh Dhakal & Jaga Basnet, *Peasant Studies in Nepal*. Kathmandu: Vajra Books.

Seddon, David. (1981). *Moroccan Peasants*. Folkestone, Kent: Wm Dawson.

Seddon, David., with Blaikie, Piers., & Cameron, John. (1979, 2001). *Peasants and Workers in Nepal*, Delhi: Vikas Publishers.

Shah, Saubhagya. (2018) *A Project of Memoreality: Transnational Development and Local Activism*. Kathmandu: Social Science Baha & Himal Books

Shrestha, P. (2032 vs, 1977). *The Manifesto of the All Nepal Peasant Association (ANPA) and its Strategies.*

Shrestha-Schipper, Satya. (2013). 'The Political Context and the Influence of the People's War in Jumla', In ed. Marie Lecomte-Tilouine. *Revolution in Nepal: an anthropological and historical approach to the People's War.* Delhi: Oxford University Press.

Singh, Mohan Bikram. (1992). *Char Dashak: Char Dashak ko Bibadha, Birodha ra Sangarsha ko Rajniti (Four Decades: four decades of controversy, opposition and struggle)*. Gorakhpur: Janashahitya Prakashan

Singh, Mohan Bikram. (2003). 'The Royal Palace Massacre and the Maoists' Pro-King Political Line'. In eds Arjun Karki & David Seddon. *The People's War in Nepal: left perspectives*, pp. 315-374.

Terray, Emmanuel. (1974). 'Long distance trade and the formation of the state: the case of the Abron kingdoms of Gyaman', *Economy & Society*, vol.3, no. 3.

Thapa, Shanker. (2001). *Peasant Insurgence in Nepal 1951-1960*. Bhaktpur: Nirmala KC.

Thapa, Shanker. (2000). *Historical Study of Agrarian Relations in Nepal (1846-1951)*, Delhi: Adroit Publishers.

Thapa, Shanker. (1996). 'An approach to the peasant movements in Nepal, 1951-1960'. *Tribhuvan University Journal*, xix, 73-88.

Thapa, Shanker. (1995). *Agrarian Relations in Nepal: owners-cultivators in a traditional agriculture*, unpubl. PhD, Patna University.

Upreti, Bishnu., Sharma, Sagar Raj., & Basnet, Jagat. (eds). (2008). *Land, Politics and Conflict in Nepal: realities and potentials for agrarian transformation.* Kathmandu: Community Self-Reliance Centre, South Asia Regional Co-ordination Office of NCCR North-South, and Human and Natural Resources Studies Centre (HNRSC), Kathmandu University.

Walton, John., & Seddon, David. (1994). *Free Markets and Food Riots: the politics of global adjustment.* Oxford: Blackwells.

Whelpton, John. (2013). 'Political Violence in Nepal from Unification to Jana Andolan I: the background to the People's War. In (ed) Marie Lecomte-Tilouine. *Revolution in Nepal: an anthropological and historical approach to the People's War.* Oxford: Oxford University Press.

Wolf, Eric. (1971). *Peasant Wars of the Twentieth Century,* London: Faber & Faber.

Index

A

B

I

J

K

L

M

N

O

P

Q

R

S

Y

Z